LEGENDARY SHOW JUMPERS

LEGENDARY SHOW JUMPERS

The Incredible Stories of
Great Canadian Horses

ANIMAL/SPORT

by Debbie Gamble-Arsenault

PUBLISHED BY ALTITUDE PUBLISHING CANADA LTD.
1500 Railway Avenue, Canmore, Alberta T1W 1P6
www.altitudepublishing.com
1-800-957-6888

Extreme care has been taken to ensure that all information presented in
this book is accurate and up to date. Neither the author nor the
publisher can be held responsible for any errors.

Publisher	Stephen Hutchings
Associate Publisher	Kara Turner
Series Editor	Jill Foran
Editors	Audrey McClellan, Jill Foran

We acknowledge the financial support of the Government
of Canada through the Book Publishing Industry Development
Program (BPIDP) for our publishing activities.

Altitude GreenTree Program
Altitude Publishing will plant twice as many trees as were used
in the manufacturing of this product.

National Library of Canada Cataloguing in Publication Data

CIP data is available on request from the publisher

ISBN: 1-55153-980-2

An application for the trademark for Amazing Stories™
has been made and the registered trademark is pending.

Printed and bound in Canada by Friesens
2 4 6 8 9 7 5 3 1

The cover photograph shows Ian Millar riding Big Ben.
(Photo by Cealy Tetley)

Dedication

For my grandmother, "Grammy Robin" (Hilda King Robinson), who read to me when I was little and always encouraged my "artistic" side.

For my parents, Jeanne and Aubrey Gamble, who raised us with love and, realizing the importance of reading, always gave us books.

For my husband, Tim Arsenault, who by showing the courage to go back to school, inspired *me* to try something new.

For my family, who've always accepted my writing, this crazy thing that I do.

And most of all, for Julie V. Watson, who befriended me, mentored me, encouraged me, and most of all, believed in me. I am forever grateful. Thank you, "Jewels" ... you are a pearl without price.

Author's Note

Throughout this book I make reference to horses being so many "hands high," commonly written as "hh." We measure the height of horses from the ground to the top of the withers — where the neck joins the shoulders — and traditionally it is done in "hands." One hand equals 4 inches or 10 centimetres; therefore, a horse said to be 16 hh would be 160 centimetres at the withers.

In addition, height is read in hands and inches, so a horse noted as 16.3 hh would be 16 hands, plus 3 inches tall, or 167.5 centimetres tall.

Contents

Prologue

As a child, you always dreamed of learning to ride and becoming a famous show jumper someday, but circumstances put that dream on the back burner. Now, however, the time is right.

You've been taking lessons from a competent and caring riding coach; you've made encouraging progress in your flat work, trotted over cavalletti poles, and even popped over some low jumps. Today's the big day: your first lesson over multiple jumps. Today you learn how to fly.

"Okay, remember what we practised," says Judy, your coach, as you tack up Spook, a flashy yet elegant bay Appaloosa gelding with a white-blanketed rump that looks like someone threw a white sheet over his hind end, then splashed it with large spots of dark brown paint.

"Begin at the walk, out along the rail. Cue him to a trot and then, in the corner, ease him into a canter, turn in, and go down the line.

"There are only three small jumps, set at one foot six inches, two feet, and two foot three," she continues.

"They're easy. Don't rush them, and don't be afraid. You can do it. I have confidence in you!"

With your heart in your throat, you do as Judy has directed, muttering all her instructions from previous lessons under your breath. Heels down, knees in, elbows close to your sides, leg aid on, reins, position ... There's so much to remember.

So far, so good. Spook has picked up a slow, controlled canter perfectly, and you turn him in towards the line of jumps. But from here they look a lot higher — more like 10 feet high than two feet. Your heart begins to pound harder, you stiffen up, and your fingers take a stranglehold on the reins as the jumps loom closer, ever closer ...

With his head weaving from one side to the other due to your uncertain guidance, Spook canters more and more slowly as he approaches the first element. At the designated take-off point, he stops, steps delicately over the first jump, stops again, and turns his head back to look at you quizzically, as if to say, "Now what?"

Embarrassed, and blushing madly, you glance shamefacedly at Judy ... and you both burst into laughter. "You were giving him mixed signals," she giggles. "Your legs were saying, 'Go on, jump,' but your mind and hands were saying, 'Stop! Stop!' With your instructions in such a muddle, Spook simply went on his own best judgment.

Prologue

"Okay, take him around and try again," Judy urges. "This time, give him a bit longer rein — don't choke him off. Keep the same amount of leg on and you'll do fine. Find the rhythm of the jumps," she points out. "Canter, canter, jump. Two strides, jump. Three strides, jump. That's all there is to it. Off you go!"

"I hope not," you mutter as you rein Spook around and trot off for the second try. Fiercely determined to get it right this time, you follow Judy's instructions and approach the first jump again, cajoling yourself, "Okay, Self, here we go. Canter, canter ..." At exactly the right moment you rise into the two-point position, move your hands up Spook's neck to give him enough rein, and suddenly you feel lighter than air.

The wind whistles past your ears. Spook's muscles bunch and flex beneath you. What power! Up and over; touch down lightly; stride, stride; aloft over the second element; stride, stride, stride; a bigger effort at jump number three, and then, all too soon, the end.

You slow your mount to a walk, beaming with pleasure as Judy applauds. You've done it. You've successfully piloted a high-flying horse over your first jump combination. What was there to be scared about? Suddenly, you realize you're hooked ...

Chapter 1
In the Beginning

Never mind that the two horses and their riders were tired, or that some dangerous ground lay between them and the ultimate goal. The honour of both men, and their belief and pride in their mounts, was at stake.

The competition started innocently enough. At the end of a long and arduous day of foxhunting, O'Callaghan and Blake had been making their way homeward. A taste of the stirrup-cup — the traditional drink offered to riders at the start of a day of hunting — had been augmented by nips from their pocket flasks throughout the day as they toasted each good draw of scent, the successful hunt, and even each other. (Truth be told, the soothing libation, the day's exertion, and the fresh air had made both the men quite tipsy, relaxed, and happy.)

O'Callaghan was well pleased with the results of the splendiferous day. His fast, brave, big-jumping Irish Mist had followed gamely right behind the Master of the Hunt all day, leaping whatever obstacle stood in his way without any refusal or second look. O'Callaghan had been close enough to the action at the end of the hunt to see the hounds finish off the fox.

Usually a nose-to-the-grindstone sort of person, O'Callaghan felt not one iota of regret at leaving his son to oversee the running of the farm. This day had given him some never-to-be-forgotten memories.

Blake was equally jubilant. He had prevented the fox from going to ground by blocking Reynard's escape route long enough for the hounds to catch him up, and for that, Blake had received the brush and mask.

The fact of the matter was that Blake and his horse, Donegal, had become separated from the field, as well as slightly lost, and had stopped to take a breather. When the fox circled back around to lose the hounds, it ended up in the same spot where the horse and rider were resting. That he had been in just the right place at just the right time more by good luck than good management was forgotten now as Blake congratulated himself on his prowess in the hunting field. For that shining moment, he had risen from being a simple farmer to become a "hard man to hounds."

As horsemen do at the end of a satisfying day, the two began to regale each other with the exploits and virtues of their respective mounts. They were ambling peaceably past Buttervent Church when O'Callaghan bragged, "And did ye see that larripin' big lep my fine Mist took at Murphy's stone wall? Sure and no other horse in the whole of Ireland could have done it better. 'Tis none so brave and fine as he." O'Callaghan leaned over and gave his horse a prideful pat on the side of the neck.

"Away with ye, O'Callaghan," Blake chided his friend. "'Twas me and my own Donegal was right on yer tail at that wall, and pullin' to pass ye, he was. 'Twere only by the grace o' God — and me own skilful ridin', mind! — that we didn't run over the pair o' ye." Donegal snorted explosively, as if to punctuate Blake's boastful statement. (One can do few worse things to an Irishman than insult his horse; both men would have done well to remember that.)

O'Callaghan pulled Mist to a halt and stared at his compatriot in amazement and outrage. "The day *yer* rack o' bones can pass *my* good-as-gold Mist, boyo, will be the day I don a petticoat 'n' curls, 'n' become a tavern wench," he jeered.

"Rack o' bones?" Blake spluttered. "Me beautiful Donnie-boy can outrun and outjump that swaybacked, bog-spavined pony of yours with a league's head start, any day, any time."

"Pony? Pony!" O'Callaghan howled, incensed, shaking his fist at the other man. Irish Mist was a robust, well-muscled blood horse, by the famous sire Armagh Warrior, a grandson of the Godolphin Arabian, out of an equally finely bred mare, and he was a strapping 16 hands into the bargain. In O'Callaghan's eyes, calling his pride and joy a *pony* was the ultimate affront.

The gauntlet had been thrown down; the matter must be resolved. Casting a look around the countryside, O'Callaghan's eyes lit on the steeple of St. Leger Church, far away across the valley. Suddenly, inspiration hit.

"All right, then," he challenged. "If yer Donegal is so bloody good, he'll not be having a problem beating me and Mist to yon church. First one there and touches the front door is the winner and has the better horse. Are ye man enough t'accept the contest?"

Blake paled and tugged at his shirt collar. St. Leger was nearly 10 miles away — and between it and Buttervent Church lay some of the hilliest, rockiest, most densely wooded land in the entire county. But he had run off at the mouth, bragging about Donegal, and now he had to pay the piper. Manfully, he faced O'Callaghan squarely and stuck out his hand.

"All right, then, shake on it," he said. And O'Callaghan did. They tightened loosened girths, gathered loose reins, and lined up side by side. The horses, which until now had been plodding along like placid old stable hacks for hire, sensed their masters' excitement and began dancing and jigging in anticipation.

"On my word, go," O'Callaghan instructed, then immediately shouted "Go!" With a great lunge, they were off.

Because O'Callaghan was the one who gave the signal to start, he got the jump on Blake and was a horse's length ahead as they cleared the first fence and thundered over the winter-dry grass of Jack Killorn's 10-acre field. Up, over, and out, galloping onward, ever onward, through meadow and field, over hill and dale. The wild grasses at the edge of the road bent at the rush of their passing, as though before the onslaught of a powerful wind.

Helter-skelter, they crossed the high road and took a huge leap over a hawthorn hedge into a rock-strewn pasture, horseshoes striking sparks off stone as they clattered forward, dodging slumbering sheep and startled lambs.

In the Beginning

Through Wharraton Wood, where a solid oak branch nearly swept Blake from the saddle when Donegal ducked under it rather than go around the tree. A covey of quail, flushed from their hiding place by the riders' yells to their horses, exploded into the air practically under Irish Mist's nose, which caused the horse a moment of panicked surprise; however, he recovered quickly and galloped strongly forward.

On and on they went, Irish Mist sometimes in front, Donegal stealing the lead at other times, but always their riders urging them, beseeching them to greater speed. The men kept their eyes glued to the steeple of St. Leger as the distance between them and their goal lessened.

Stirrup to stirrup, they charged through a gate and across the expanse of a hayfield. They cleared the dry-stone wall that marked the field's boundaries, and as they did — in mid-jump in fact — O'Callaghan was horrified to discover that what lay beyond the wall was a sprightly babbling brook, glistening in the weak winter sun and burbling joyously as it tumbled over its rocky bed. Its watery laughter sounded like hoots of derision and doom in O'Callaghan's ears. If Irish Mist had a fault, it was that he hated getting his feet wet and would do anything to avoid it. In that split second between discovery and disaster, O'Callaghan braced himself for the inevitable.

Irish Mist saw the brook, performed the equine equivalent of a double-take, and then twisted himself in midair, loath to land in the brook. With superlative effort — and a large dose of luck — he cleared the brook but stumbled on landing, nearly falling to his knees. O'Callaghan was yanked out of the saddle and almost over Mist's ears. Donegal surged ahead, and Blake yelled, "Be seein' ya at church, boyo!" as the pair fled away towards the ultimate goal.

After a brief but taxing struggle, O'Callaghan managed to drag himself back into the saddle, while his gallant horse regained his feet and resumed the chase. Blake and Donegal were many lengths ahead, but Irish Mist was nothing if not game, and he resumed the powerful rhythm of his gallop as he put his all into catching up to the disappearing Donegal. "Come on, me lovely, come on," O'Callaghan crooned and cajoled, flattening himself along Mist's neck as the wind rushed past. "Ye can do it, I know ye can."

By now, exhausted muscles were protesting, overtaxed lungs were heaving, and every stride was an effort. But the hot blood of competitive horses coursed through Irish Mist's veins, and he was as arrogant as he was fast and beautiful. Coming in second was unthinkable; getting his nose in front was all. He pinned back his ears, stretched out his neck, stuck out his muzzle, levelled out even more with his ground-eating stride, and refused to give in.

Blake looked back in dismay as O'Callaghan and Mist bore down on him and Donegal. Their opponents were only four horse-lengths behind, then three, moving ever closer with vengeful purpose, like one of the four horsemen of the Apocalypse. The power and grace of Mist's stride was a fearful thing to see.

Frantically, Blake gave his horse a sharp tap with the whip, and Donegal gallantly responded with yet another burst of speed. But Irish Mist would not be denied.

With three great bounds, he caught up to Donegal and then stubbornly won back the lead, inch by painful inch. He was a neck ahead of Donegal as they cleared the boundary fence into the churchyard, scattering gaping villagers in all directions as a fox scatters pullets in a henhouse. With one final spectacular leap, Irish Mist skidded to a halt at the front of the church as O'Callaghan leaned far out of the saddle to give the door a triumphant slap. "We win!" he gasped, exultant, as Donegal slid to a stop practically on Mist's heels.

Both horses stood, spraddle-legged, heads low, ears at half mast, and sides heaving. Equally spent, the two men oozed from their saddles and sat on the church doorstep to regain their breath and composure. When they could finally speak, Blake ruefully offered his hand to O'Callaghan and said, "I concede, my friend. Your horse *is* better than mine."

"Thank ye fer sayin' that, friend. Mist *did* do well, didn't he?" said O'Callaghan, basking in the glory of victory and the admiration of his friend. "But ye gave it a fine try, Blake. My hat's off to ye and Donegal both. Between us, we've the two best horses in the whole of Ireland.

"Now, let's be gettin' these laddies home t'some bran mash and a warm stable," he said with a soft laugh as he struggled, groaning, to his feet and prepared to remount. "They both deserve t'be treated like royalty ..."

High-Flying Facts

The previous account is a work of fiction from the imagination of the author. Only the names of the men and the churches are real. The story does reflect, however, the truth about the origins of the steeplechase. Riders and their hunting horses had to learn to jump all manner of different types of fences when British farmland began to be enclosed in the 18th century. Attention to bloodlines and breeding resulted in faster horses, which naturally led to disputes over the speed and ability of those horses.

These disputes were often settled by running

match races across the countryside. Since churches were very visible landmarks, they were often used as start and finish points for these impromptu races, which were dubbed steeplechases. In 1752, a Mr. Blake and a Mr. O'Callaghan raced each other from Buttervent Church to St. Leger Church in Ireland.

In 1810, Bedlam, England was the site of the first race ever recorded over a prepared steeplechase course with fences made specifically for that purpose. The granddaddy of all steeplechases, the Grand National Steeplechase, was established at Liverpool, England in 1837.

The wild thrills of a steeplechase race were obviously addictive, because the sport was eventually brought to North America in the early 19th century.

The Mists of Time

No one knows precisely when humans started riding horses over high jumps, but we do know that an attraction for the thrill of flying through the air with a good horse under you surfaced early in our equine history.

Foxhunting has been around for thousands of years. Alexander the Great (356–323 B.C.) took time out from his many war campaigns to enjoy foxhunting in parts of Asia, and Persian history records show foxhunting on horseback was taking place by 4 B.C. Foxhunting with hounds is recorded to have happened in both Thrace (now Istanbul, Turkey) and Italy by about A.D. 80. British officers, enthusiastic about their horses and hunting, took the sport with them wherever they went. The colonization of foreign countries under the British crown required that the British army be in residence. Consequently, British officers were largely responsible for the spread of foxhunting traditions to Africa, New Zealand, Australia, and India, where, instead of foxes, they hunted the fox's cousin, the jackal.

The arrival in Maryland of Robert Brooke, his family, and his hounds on June 30, 1650, is the earliest report of hounds being imported to North America. An avid hunter from the age of 16, George Washington owned both an excellent pack of hounds and a stable of finely bred horses to enable him to enjoy his passion. Thomas Jefferson was also an ardent foxhunting aficionado.

Embraced by nearly every part of America, the sport became most popular in the mid-south, which had maintained many of the aristocratic English traditions and still had large, unfenced land masses ideally suited for the chase.

The Montreal Hunt was the first foxhound club in Canada; it was established in 1826. The first steeplechase organized in North America was also held in the area of Montreal. The Montreal Steeplechase course of 1840 was three miles long, featuring numerous brooks and 20 obstacles.

Why Do They Do It?

Who could deny the attraction of an exhilarating day on horseback, a staggering variety and number of fences taken at speed, and the sheer joy of spending time with your favourite mount, in the company of others who enjoy riding as much as you do?

Foxhunting is horses, hounds, and humans in blissful partnership, revelling in the exhilaration of searching out one of the most cunning creatures in the animal kingdom, while enjoying Nature's beauty. Riding the horse allows man to keep pace with the hounds as they seek their quarry. The rider is party to the sights, smells, and sounds of the hunt: the streaking rust-red blur of the fox, pursued by the black, white, and tan-coloured pack; the rich, earthy smell of the ground, the trees, and the fields; and the deep, full-bodied baying of the hounds, accompanied by the thunder of many hooves and the brassy sound of the huntsman's horn as it echoes over hill and dale. No two chases are the same, and every new hunt is a unique experience.

An old poem called "The Fox and the Owl," by that great writer Anonymous, also illustrates the romance of chasing a wily fox high, wide, and handsome over the picturesque countryside. This poem was handed down to me by my maternal grandfather, Nelson H. Robinson (1902–1995), who learned it at *his* grandmother's knee.

> *But I'll tell Jack, with his hounds and his horn ...*
> *And the bow-wow dogs, and the toot-toot horn,*
> *and the galloping horse, and Jack*
> *Will race you and trace you wherever they chase*
> *you, and thunder along your track.*
>
> *So the next morning, out came Jack, with his*
> *spurs on his heels, and his whip to crack,*
> *And saddled his horse, and called for his pack,*
> *and started off on the fox's track.*
> *Away they went with the clattering sound of the*
> *swift-footed horse on the frosty ground,*
> *And the horn that rang with a merry sound,*
> *and the deep-mouthed bay of the hunting hound.*
> *With the "toot-y-too" of their horn that blew,*
> *they made such a noise as on they flew*
> *That the old fox didn't know what to do ...*

Jump To It

The sport of show jumping developed nearly 100 years after steeplechasing and could be called a "new" sport, by comparison. A harness show hosted in Paris, France, in 1866 held a class for jumpers. Early jumping shows would have competitors parade in the show ring, then ride across country for the jumping portion of the contest. Because this type of show wasn't very interesting for spectators, the organizers began setting the jumps up inside the arena. These events were known not as jumping competitions, but as "lepping."

The Royal Dublin Society hosted the first official show-jumping competition in Ireland in 1864. Horses had to jump only three obstacles: a stone wall, a brush-and-rails combination, and a long jump over hurdles.

By about 1881, lepping had spread to Britain, and by 1900, most of the higher calibre shows included the classes in their program. When British military officers and regiments were stationed in Canada, they quite naturally continued the equestrian activities in which they participated at home: racing, polo, steeplechasing, and foxhunting. By 1900, these "horse games" all had a firm foothold in this country.

It seems only natural, then, that the first competition teams were made up of military men. In 1909, a Canadian team of three horse/rider combinations went to the first Nations Cup in Olympia, England. They finished in fourth place.

Until 1948, only military riders were eligible to

compete at international equestrian team events. In that year, the rule requiring competitors to be military personnel was abolished, making way for men of either "professional" or "amateur" status to compete. (Riders are considered to be professional if they are over 18 years of age and train horses for sale, give riding lessons, train or board horses, or show them for pay. Amateurs are riders over the age of 18 who do not get paid for riding or working with horses.) It was 1956 before women were allowed to ride on Olympic Nations Cup teams.

Things have changed in the past 50 years. Although there are still some military riders, who compete in uniform, the sport is dominated by civilian men and women, who compete against each other on equal terms. Oddly enough, most riders are professionals in that they give lessons or train horses to sell them, but are considered amateurs for the Olympics.

Horses and Courses
The objective of show jumping is for the horse-and-rider team to complete a course of jumps without incurring penalties by knocking down a rail or any part of the jump combinations. This takes a horse of supreme ability, one that can jump high enough to clear triple bars or parallel rails, and wide enough to cover a spread such as "stone" walls, water jumps, or combinations of any

of the aforementioned obstacles.

The horse must also be fast, as there is a time limit for jumping the course. A horse/rider combination receives penalties (or faults, as they are called in the sport) if they exceed the time allowed or if the horse refuses to jump an obstacle. In addition, if they fall, or if they take the jumps in the wrong order, the horse and rider are eliminated.

When two or more horses in the same competition go clean (with no faults), they enter a "jump-off." Should they all go clean again, the winner will be the one who has completed the course in the fastest time.

In a regular jumping class there is a set number of obstacles. The horse must jump over them in a specified order, within a prescribed time limit.

However, there are almost as many kinds of jumping competitions as there are horses to enter them. In the Puissance, the goal is to see who can jump the highest. The Parcours de Chasse is a speed class, won by the fastest time. Each knockdown adds time to the final score, instead of faults. The Grand Prix tests the horses' athleticism with obstacles from four feet six inches to five feet three inches high, and spreads of six feet six inches.

Mostly, horses and riders compete as individuals. Sometimes, however, they are part of a team, often representing their country in a Nations Cup or the Olympics, and the scores of three or four horses on a team are added together. The team with the lowest score wins.

In a Scurry class, horses compete simultaneously. Two identical courses are set up and horses jump-off in heats, with the winner of each heat advancing to the next round until an overall winner is declared.

Then there are specialty jumping classes like the Gambler's Choice or the Equine/Canine Challenge held at the Royal Winter Fair in Toronto. In the Gambler's Choice, each jump is assigned a point value. The harder the jump, the more points it is worth, with the Joker fence being worth the maximum 200 points. Riders are allowed to jump the fences from either direction and in any order. They try to clear as many as they can in the allotted time of 45 seconds. The rider with the highest point total wins.

The Royal show program explains the Equine/Canine Challenge this way: "The performing dogs are teamed up with an open jumper in this class. It is a relay race where the dogs race through their obstacles and then the horses have to negotiate their course. Both dogs and horses are timed and penalties are given for refusals and knockdowns."

No matter what type of jumping competition is

mentioned, Canadians can point with pride to the horses that carry their country's flag to the winner's circle. What follows are the unofficial biographies of just a few of the best our history has to offer.

Chapter 2
High-Flying Forefathers

igh-flying horses have been a big part of Canadian history. Fantastic jumping horses set early records and made their marks for other horses to aim at. The horses whose stories are related in this chapter did not compete against each other. Their lives merely overlapped at the edges: the last years in the life of one were often the first years in the life of another.

Some of them were fine-blooded, purebred horses; others had parentage that was, to put it mildly, interesting. Some were on the show circuit for many years; others for only a few. Their lives span the years 1912 to

1971, but collectively, they reigned supreme in the show-jumping world as some of the finest examples of high-flying Canadian horses.

To Set Records, You Just Need Confidence

The year was 1912; the place, the National Horse Show in New York. Colonel Clifford Sifton (who was knighted in 1915 to become Sir Clifford) had brought his horse Confidence — piloted by Jack Hamilton, a professional rider — to the competition. Along with numerous other owners, Sifton aspired to win the title of high-jumping champion, and he had confidence in Confidence's talent.

Sifton's bay gelding was of questionable ancestry, but he was thought to be part Hackney, part who knows what. The horse was born in 1899 near Cobourg, Ontario, and eventually came into the Crowe & Murray stables in Toronto.

At a height of close to 16 hh, with a powerful, thick-set body, Confidence's action was accented by the white sock on his near hind leg. In riders' terms, he "filled the eye," and it was most likely his presence and looks that prompted a Mr. Matthews of Toronto to buy Confidence, along with a matching animal, to be used as a carriage pair.

In an ideal carriage horse, the sought-after gaits are a brisk walk, an animated yet low-speed trot, and a faster gait called the strong trot or road-trot. Cantering in harness is frowned on — but someone neglected to acquaint Confidence with this fact. When the new owner took delivery of his equine pair and put them to work, he found that Confidence "mixed his gaits" (probably meaning he cantered instead of road-trotting). Back he and his harness mate went to Crowe & Murray. Oh, the shame! Traded in for a more suitable candidate.

At the time, there were not enough heavy hunters to meet the market demand, so Jim Murray, one of the partners in the stable, resolved to test Confidence for that sector of the market. Putting the gelding over some practice fences, Murray found that Confidence had some "jump" in him, and it wasn't long before Captain W.T. Evans of Montreal bought the sturdy fellow.

While Evans owned him, Confidence was part of a team that went to the International Horse Show at Olympia, in London, England, and competed in the International Challenge Cup, featuring an award donated by King Edward VII. The event called for clearing 11 jumps in two minutes and was considered very difficult for that era. Vying for the prize against army officers from Italy and Belgium, the Canadian team, although skilful, was denied the win.

As an individual entry, however, Confidence did much better. On July 1, 1909, the *London Free Press* broadcast that Confidence had cleared a jump of seven feet, triumphing over Jubilee, a French entry, who had unsuccessfully attempted a jump of six feet eight inches.

His stellar performance brought Confidence to the attention of Clifford Sifton, who promptly purchased him. Sifton also lured away Jack Hamilton, who had been the rider/horse trainer for Crowe & Murray.

No doubt this continuity in training played a large part in Confidence's future successes; in addition to being consistent winners in Canadian events, the horse/rider combination triumphed in the National Horse Show high-jump competitions in New York in both 1910 and 1911.

But it was in 1912 that Confidence's star shone brightest, for it was then, at the very same National Horse Show in New York, that he outdid himself. Each one of the competitors, in their turn, jumped their best — but their best was not good enough. Each one tried, and each one failed.

Confidence entered the ring. The crowd was focused on the bouncing bay campaigner, wondering if the obstacle would defeat him as it had done the horses that had come before him.

The rapid-fire beat of his hooves echoed as the gelding moved towards the jump. He heaved himself into the air, reaching, stretching, straining towards the rafters on his ascent to the summit of the barrier before him.

Sprightly as a deer, Confidence took to the air and sprang mightily over the top bar — and it stayed up! Not only had he outstripped all other entries, he also set the astounding record of eight feet and half an inch, a high-jump record that stood for over a decade.

It was a record not without controversy, however. An American horseman named Dick Donnelly had a horse called Heatherbloom at home on his farm in Richmond, Virginia. Donnelly claimed this horse had jumped eight feet two inches in 1902. He even had photographs of this supposed jump taking place on his farm property. But because Heatherbloom's jump hadn't been officially recorded, the mark set by Confidence remained on the books until 1923, when the American horse Great Heart jumped eight feet and thirteen-sixteenths of an inch in Chicago.

Confidence, meanwhile, had been sold to a riding school in Brooklyn, New York, in 1914, at the start of World War I. In 1915, during his stay there, Marie-Louise Thompson, who rode in a sidesaddle, took him over a seven-foot jump.

It's not uncommon for good horses to change hands often, to be bought and sold a lot. It's also not uncommon for people to buy back a horse that they've sold earlier. Perhaps the Siftons really missed their old companion, for he returned to his home at their stables a few years later. The gallant 22-year-old campaigner made a farewell appearance at the Canadian National Exhibition in 1921. In 1923, Confidence died and was laid to rest in Gormley, Ontario, on the Siftons' Foxton Farm.

The talented highflyer had lived a long life as a strong competitor with an illustrious career, staving off challenges to his supremacy for many years. He remained at the top of the heap for a period of years longer than some horses live!

Assurance in Confidence's ability as a high flyer had never been misplaced.

Air Pilot, Not for the Faint of Heart

Canada's prairie provinces are proud of their cowboy heritage, of which good, honest western horses are an unforgettable part. However, one of the most memorable horses in prairie history was not a cow pony at all, but a dynamic jumping horse named Air Pilot.

Air Pilot was a square peg in a round hole. A black Standardbred, destined by heredity and tradition to be a harness horse, he changed his destiny by the very force of his attitude and a boundless zest for competition.

He was born in 1933, during the Great Depression and in the middle of a drought, eking out an existence on not much more than Russian thistle. Despite the meagre diet, he matured into a handsome young horse and was broken for use in harness.

Unfortunately for his owners (but propitiously for him), Air Pilot was not enamoured of the standard sedate jog of a regular farm or ranch wagon horse; he wanted to race with the wind! Most farmers and ranchers of that era were more concerned with the race for survival than with racing fast horses for entertainment, but Dr. N.V. James, a veterinarian from Regina, was travelling through the area and happened to see the well-developed gelding. Dr. James was a connoisseur of fine horseflesh, so when he first glimpsed Air Pilot, he was captivated by the horse's conformation, powerful muscles, fearless manner, and above all, blazing speed. Dr. James was determined to buy this epitome of equine perfection. In 1941, $75 was a lot of money, and the former owners were convinced to part with their previously unappreciated speed-demon.

Air Pilot went into training to become a jumping horse as soon as Dr. James got him to Regina. Although he was courageous from the outset, he was quite a klutz and knocked down as many jumps as he successfully cleared. Amazingly, he never refused a jump, no matter how unlikely it was that he'd get over it. This talent was encouraging.

For every yin there's a yang, and for every silver lining there's a cloud. The cloud looming on Air Pilot's horizon was that, in spite of his admirable talent, he got fiercely impatient as soon as he saw a jumping obstacle. Immediately, the desire to jump outstripped his responsiveness to guidance from his rider. As soon as the word "go" was given, he was like a runaway locomotive hurtling towards the jump.

Despite appearances, a rider does not just go along for the ride. He or she is a vital part of the partnership, making sure the horse is at the correct take-off point to make a successful jump, neither too close to the obstacle nor too far away. The rider also tells the horse to shorten or lengthen the stride for the distances between hurdles, alerts the animal to whether they're about to scale a vertical or spread element, and guides the horse around the course to ensure he takes the jumps in the proper order.

Being Air Pilot's rider was not for the faint of heart. Because of the gelding's impetuousness, riding him was a game of chance, wavering between triumph and disaster. It was a toss-up whether he'd decide to crash through the jump or go over it.

As Air Pilot's training progressed, his jumping improved. However, no amount of training diminished the reckless abandon with which he careened around a jumping course like a demented steamroller.

He was always extremely popular with spectators because no one ever knew from one of his appearances to the next whether he would demolish the jumps, go perfectly clear, or forsake the course, jump the ringside barriers, and join them in the stands, which apparently happened on more than one occasion. Even Air Pilot himself was never sure what the day would bring — but come what may, he was consistently enthusiastic.

One might think that riding this kamikaze pony would be akin to suicide, but most of his riders — a large number of them young women — came through the experience unscathed. They had great confidence in the horse, secure in the knowledge that he might totally annihilate an obstacle, but he would never ever come to a skidding, disastrous halt or duck out before the jump.

There were a great many popular jumpers travelling the show circuit in those days. It seemed that every major city had its equine hero, and spectators at the shows were treated to battles for show-jumping supremacy between them. Brandon had Bouncing Buster, Calgary had Cool Customer, Winnipeg had Copper King ... and then, of course, there was that Pilot horse from Regina. The crowds cheered all fine performers, and Air Pilot received his share of adulation, being a fine campaigner who never disappointed his fans.

High-Flying Forefathers

Sometimes a winner, sometimes a loser, but always a sensation, Air Pilot travelled the show circuit year after year. So what if he didn't always win the show champion's trophy? Scores of show-jumping fans loved and admired his unfailing spirit and courage. They knew that if Air Pilot was on the roster, they would see a *real* show!

In the show ring, Pilot acted like a raving lunatic, as wild as the winds of a hurricane. Few people knew that once out of the limelight and back in his stall, he was a model equine citizen, gentle and quiet. All they saw was the fire and demonic tendencies he exhibited within the ring, so he never captured the level of public loyalty that some of his competitors did.

Air Pilot performed in many show rings, in towns all over the West. The best jump he ever made took place at a show in Calgary. It isn't recorded just who he was competing against, or how many other jumpers were in the class. Neither do we know if he had to complete a whole course of jumps, or whether the object of the exercise was to go for height over just one obstacle. What we can be sure of is that Air Pilot gave it his best shot, just like always. Was he fractious going into the ring? Probably. Did his rider's arms ache from the strain of trying to rein in the frenzied four-legged fury beneath him? Most likely.

Perhaps eyewitnesses to the event would have told you that Air Pilot went from a semi-controlled cavort to a nearly out-of-control bound towards the fence, with his rider clinging on like a burr. The force and speed of the horse's stride caused a wind that whipped his mane about his head in stinging tendrils. Bearing down on the barrier with vengeful purpose, Pilot's strong hind legs thrust him into the air and he rose powerfully towards the top bar. Everyone was breathless with anticipation. Come on, come on ...

Like a tornado clearing everything in its path, Air Pilot cleared the apex of the jump. He flew over the top, set at six feet four inches, and in so doing, posted a personal best height. As well, it was the highest jump ever cleared by a Saskatchewan horse.

Air Pilot was officially retired at the Calgary Horse Show in 1955. The organizers erected a jump pegged at six feet four inches to illustrate his greatest achievement. The plan was for Barney Williams, who had co-piloted the gelding over that highest jump, to ride him around the arena while the commentator explained that it was Pilot's last appearance before retiring to green pastures and a life of idle luxury. But once again, the quirky equine upset the apple cart.

At the time, Air Pilot was 22 in body, but much younger in mind. When he was ridden into the ring and saw the demonstration jump, it was all Williams could do to restrain the horse from trying to spring over it.

Four thousand spectators were on hand for the special event, and so were the top riders who had ridden Pilot at one show or another, nearly a dozen in all. While organ music swelled above his head, the "grand old man" was adorned with a wreath of flowers and received wave upon wave of applause as he took the out-gate for the last time.

Air Pilot and Dr. James, his owner, retired together on Vancouver Island, enjoying their golden years until Dr. James passed away in 1959. Shortly thereafter, Air Pilot followed, making his final flight.

Pinnacle, the High-Flying Houdini

A few horsemen have one in their barns; many don't. Those who have them, often curse them. Those who don't have them are lucky. Some owners affectionately refer to them as "characters"; others refer to them, not so affectionately, as a bloody nuisance. What are they? Equine escape artists, unofficially known as "Houdini horses."

They come in all breeds, shapes, ages, and sizes, and you never know that you have one until it's too late, and the beast is home in your barn. Be prepared: these skilful scamps can undo, untie, unlatch, or unfasten any rope, snap, button, or hook that mere humans devise.

Pinnacle, a seven-eighths Thoroughbred and high flyer extraordinaire, had an escape technique that would have done Harry Houdini proud. There was no malice in Pinnacle — he didn't do it to be bad; he just liked to have fun. Escaping was a challenge, and he couldn't resist a challenge, whether in the show ring or at home in the barn.

When Cliff Ross of Edmonton, Alberta, purchased Pinnacle in 1957, he had no idea what an eccentric equine he had acquired. Ross was simply looking for a competition horse for his daughter, Gail.

Like most professional athletes, Pinnacle was a serious and skilful competitor, but he wasn't all business. He liked to enjoy his relaxation time, too. Pinnacle was the alpha male in the Rosses' stable, and the family quickly learned his habits and preferences. His penchant for "going walkabout" was an entertaining quirk in his otherwise straightforward personality. That didn't lessen the pandemonium that ensued whenever Pinnacle took a notion into his head to liven up a quiet night among the stalls.

It was not uncommon for a stable hand to come to the barn and find that every box stall was open, and that the freed horses had made a spectacular mess. And who would, invariably, be standing in his own box stall, looking oh so nonchalant and innocent? The one responsible for the multiple breakout: Pinnacle.

The rapport that developed between Pinnacle and his rider would be the envy of any horseman. It stood them in good stead, and they racked up win after win, year after year. By 1961, the pair had competed successfully in shows all over Eastern Canada and on the fall show circuit in the U.S. as well. Even more eventfully, the accolades they received drew the attention of the Canadian Equestrian Team, and Gail Ross was selected for a place on the team — the first rider from Western Canada, as well as the first junior to achieve that distinction.

Pinnacle and his rider were so in tune with each other that they were like two halves of a whole being, a complete and cohesive unit, intimately aware of each other's strengths and weaknesses. This was no more aptly demonstrated than in 1961.

Mere days before the Canadian team was leaving to participate in an international event, Ross sustained a broken jaw, concussion, and fractured skull in a car accident. Her injuries were so grievous that doctors seriously doubted whether she would ever be able, or even want, to ride again.

Remarkably, she recovered quickly enough to be discharged from hospital only three weeks later, and began riding the stalwart Pinnacle soon afterwards. These actions speak more loudly of Pinnacle's great character than words ever could.

International show jumping is a highly competitive sport. When equestrians, especially those of international calibre, are injured, they do their darnedest to heal and get back to their chosen profession quickly. They don't want to do anything to jeopardize their chances or delay their return to the circuit, because if they're not competing, they're not in the hunt for the prize money.

Gail Ross's swift return to riding and competing was testimony that she had boundless faith in Pinnacle, trusting that he would take care of her and not cause her any further harm. Later that same year, the horse and rider won the Canadian Jumping Championship at the Royal Winter Fair. In 1963, they captured the New York Grand Prix, following a thrilling jump-off. They were also the North American open jumping champions of 1963. To top off their winning streak, they went to England, where they garnered even more prizes.

Pinnacle's exemplary career spanned 15 years, until his retirement in 1972 at the Northlands Horse Show in Edmonton. Spectators gave him a standing ovation as Gail Ross Amdam rode Pinnacle into the show ring to receive his due.

He was probably confused when, rather than directing him at some obstacles, Ross Amdam rode him to centre ring, where he was accented by a blazing spotlight. As a farewell anthem, a bugler played "The Last Post." Pinnacle was unsaddled and then covered with a horse blanket, topped off by a horseshoe-shaped wreath of roses.

Pinnacle, the high-flying Houdini, was returned to the Rosses' farm and a retirement of ease. In his career, he had travelled multiple miles, won numerous awards and titles, and, through it all, had earned a spot in the hearts of those who recognized his honesty, courage, and character.

Packaged Neatly With a Blue Beau

Puissance. The French word means "power" or "strength." The Puissance is to equestrian jumping what the pole vault is to track and field. As long as horses keep jumping "clean" (without refusals or knockdowns), officials keep raising the bar. And that's the stuff from which records are made and legends are born. One such legend was Blue Beau.

His rider, Tom Gayford, was a stockbroker by profession, but (more importantly) he was also a very competitive horseman, with a long list of achievements under his saddle. For instance, he was named

Champion Rider at the National Horse Show in 1958 and was part of the Canadian show-jumping team that wowed spectators with its riding prowess at the Royal Winter Fair in Toronto in 1960.

Blue Beau was owned by Mr. and Mrs. E. Herbert Coad of Aurora, Ontario. The Coads had loaned the talented bay gelding to the Canadian Equestrian Team, and he was paired with Tom Gayford. The two remained a competitive team for 11 years, amassing an incredible number of milestone wins during that time.

One of the most memorable moments was when they established a new Puissance world record at the National Horse Show in New York. A series of photographs in the book *Canada's International Equestrians* shows how much effort goes into breaking a world record. The six-photo sequence shows Gayford and Blue Beau throughout the execution of the jump: before, during, and after. Can you imagine what a radio announcer might have said on the momentous day, as he was describing the action?

"Ladies and gentlemen, in the ring now are Tom Gayford and his mount, Blue Beau. The jump has been raised to seven feet one inch. No one has jumped this height clean yet, but this pair will give it their best shot.

"The jump is a fake-stone wall, flanked on both sides by multi-coloured 'wings' — a formidable and intimidating obstacle in anyone's eyes. This capacity crowd is hushed, as horse and rider begin their warm-up circle ... and there they go!

"Gayford and Blue Beau race towards the jump. All we can see of Beau behind the jump is his ears. If he doesn't jump, it will be a horrible impact. There ... at the final second, Blue Beau has sprung powerfully off his hind legs — see how Gayford steadies the horse by supporting Beau's head as he lifts into the air.

"The horse is soaring over the obstacle. Gayford sits motionless, yet forward, skilfully aiding and guiding his mount while not upsetting his balance. It looks promising, folks.

"Beau snaps his front legs up tight to his belly, keeping them away from the jump. As he glides smooth-ly over, he extends his hind legs w-a-y back and kicks them into the air behind him as his front hooves reach the ground. With all four feet back on Mother Earth, Beau speeds away as Gayford looks back in joy and disbelief.

"Hurray! They've done it! Ladies and gentlemen, Tom Gayford and the gallant Blue Beau have triumphed in the Puissance and set a new world record of seven feet one inch here at the National Horse Show. What a night!"

New York was the scene of a series of Puissance victories for Blue Beau and Gayford. In 1960 they won, by posting a clean round three times in a row, at Madison Square Gardens. In 1961, the Puissance Wagstaff Challenge Trophy was theirs, and they assisted in a team triumph, too. It was in 1962, in repeating a Wagstaff Challenge Trophy victory, that they set the seven feet one inch Puissance record. Finally, in 1963, they won the Wagstaff for the third time, retiring the trophy.

Blue Beau's friend and rider, Tom Gayford, retired from international competition after 1968, but his expertise didn't leave the sport. He designed the show-jumping courses at the Montreal Olympics in 1976, and from 1980 through 1994 he was the Canadian team's chef d'équipe (standard industry name for a team manager). Gayford was also a member of the Canadian Equestrian Federation's national show-jumping team selection committee, and coach to his daughter, Marge Sproule.

Blue Beau continued to compete in high-flying competitions until 1965, when he was retired at the Royal Winter Fair in a special ceremony. In 1971, at the age of 23, Blue Beau died at home on the Coads' Farm in Aurora. He is buried on the farm.

Other horses jumped well, but this humble gelding always did it up fancy, with a Blue Beau.

Chapter 3
The Quest for Olympic Gold

The rules of the game are simple: jump big obstacles — lots of them. Clean. As fast as you can. Olympic show jumping is the ultimate test of a horse and rider, and nothing raises the profile of a horse/rider combination more than being able to say that they've won a medal at the Olympics.

Not many Olympic sports allow women and men to compete on equal terms, but the three equestrian disciplines — three-day eventing, dressage, and jumping — do. Moreover, the horse and rider pair are considered a team, displaying the traits of agility, daring, speed, and grace, traits that take years to perfect. At the

Olympics, feats of perfection in equestrian events often translate into gold medals.

Dressage is the supreme test of a horse's responsiveness to his rider, demanding competitors follow a set pattern of gaits and exacting movements with the rider using only the natural aids of hands, legs, and seat position to direct the horse. The Lipizzan horses of the Spanish Riding School in Austria are famous for their performances featuring many high-level dressage movements.

Three-day eventing, according to Equine Canada, "is the 'iron man' of equestrian disciplines, in which horse and rider complete three distinct tests of stamina and skill — a dressage test, a cross-country course and a stadium jumping course." A cross-country course includes two sets of roads and tracks (usually covered at a trot; the first to warm up the horse and the second as a breather between the steeplechase and cross-country), a short steeplechase course (done at a gallop over not-too-difficult jumps), and the cross-country section itself, with big, solid fences. As Equine Canada says, "A successful three-day event horse must be capable of suppleness and relaxation in the dressage test; speed, endurance and jumping ability in the cross-country course; and suppleness, obedience and energy in the stadium jumping test."

Canadian equestrians first participated in the Olympic three-day event at Helsinki in 1952, and from then on, they have never looked back.

The Road To the Medals
Team members Walter Pady, Stewart Treviranus, Tom Gayford, John Rumble, and Larry McGuinness had been training in Badminton, England, site of a famous three-day event, for six weeks before they carried the Canadian flag into Olympic equestrian battle at Helsinki.

Unfortunately, fate did not smile kindly on their high-flying endeavours. Rumble became very sick, and Pady's horse, Rocket, suffered a hock injury just after arriving in Helsinki, which meant that two of Canada's horse/rider pairs were unable to take part in the competition at all.

But the competition started off hopefully for the others. Their horses completed the first-day dressage tests competently and were passed to compete in cross-country on the second day.

The cross-country phase was no walk in the park. It included a steeplechase course that was 2.5 miles long and a cross-country course with 35 jumps in a 4.5-mile stretch. The total distance was 23 miles.

The gruelling course claimed a Canadian "victim" when Gayford, riding Constellation, came to grief at the

29th obstacle and was eliminated. McGuinness and Treviranus both completed the cross-country day without problems.

Only those who had finished the cross-country phase and had been okayed by a veterinarian could compete in the stadium jumping, held on the third day. By this time, 23 of the original 59 contestants had been eliminated. Of the 36 remaining, nine turned in clear rounds. McGuinness and Treviranus were among those nine, posting the fastest times of all: 103.6 seconds and 106.75 seconds, respectively.

Although Treviranus and McGuinness finished with no faults in both the stadium jumping and cross-country phases, neither scored high enough to be in the medals. Treviranus, riding Rustum, was ranked 22nd, while McGuinness, on Tara, was pinned in 29th place.

For the competitors — and for Canadian fans — it was a disappointing first-time showing, but better days lay ahead.

If At First You Don't Succeed ...

The world first sat up and took notice of Canadian high-jumping horses and their riders in 1956, when the Canadian team competed in the three-day event at Stockholm, Sweden. (The 1956 summer games were held in Australia, but because of the tough quarantine rules — horses shipping in had to be kept isolated for four weeks — the equestrian events were held in Sweden.)

The road to the games began with an arduous selection process. From Regina, a young farmer named Robin Hahn applied to train with the Olympic three-day-event team. Hahn had been practically born in the saddle, riding his pony to and from school, playing horse games on the prairie, and competing in horse shows as he got older. When he was notified that the three-day-event team had accepted his application, he loaded his mare, Colette, on the back of a pickup truck and headed east.

John Rumble, who had been on the team but was too ill to compete for Canada at the Helsinki Olympics, had a young friend who he thought would make a likely candidate for the '56 team. The young man's name was Jim Elder. Rumble said Elder was "jump crazy."

Another prospective team member was Brian Herbinson, a young horseman of Irish lineage in his early 20s. The Irish have been known, down through the ages, as a "horse mad" lot, so Herbinson may have been genetically disposed to compete in the Olympic equestrian events.

When the selection was concluded, the team members were Herbinson, Rumble, and Elder, with Colonel

Charles Baker as team manager, and McGuinness as non-riding team captain. Hahn went along to help out. Horses Tara, Cilroy, and Colleen were the equine partners in the endeavour, with a horse named Steelworker as a spare.

As they had done four years earlier, the Canadians trained at the facilities in Badminton before the competition. This proved beneficial, especially to Cilroy, who had been prone to rush his jumps. The training period taught him to slow down and be more cautious. The Olympic team horses and riders even competed in a one-day event at Sherborne, Dorset, before leaving for the Olympics.

In the van on the way to the airport prior to their flight to Stockholm, Cilroy was hurt. He had a cut above his hock, which became bruised and hugely swollen. The team was very concerned about the injury, not only for the horse's sake, but also because no changes in mount were allowed after a horse had been declared for the competition. If a horse or rider became sick or injured, the team would be disqualified. Fortunately, Cilroy recovered enough to pass the veterinary check and was allowed to start.

Unbelievable Hurdles
The men and horses had trained hard, and between

them they had countless years of experience in the jumping field. Despite all their training and experience, though, they couldn't believe the size and composition of the Olympic cross-country course. Oil drums, tables, chairs, umbrellas — all were employed in jump construction, combined with wide spreads and tall jumps guaranteed to tax the skill of both horse and rider to the utmost. One example that gives an indication of the severity of the course was the log jump. A horse negotiating this jump would drop four feet into water, which was two feet deep, then had to scale another wall, four feet high, to get back out. And there were 33 of these unbelievable hurdles in all.

The day of the cross-country competition, it poured rain. In spite of the inclement weather and the almost-insurmountable obstacles, the Canadians persevered, and their perseverance was rewarded. They earned a bronze medal and came home to Canada to a hero's welcome.

They were greeted at the airport by a crowd of enthusiastic supporters, and Canadian newspapers printed banner headlines about the win. Major General and Mrs. C.C. Mann — who at one time owned the famous Joker's Hill farm near King, Ontario — hosted a gala dinner party in their honour. The dinner menus were illustrated with head studies of Colleen, Tara, and

Cilroy engraved under the Olympic rings, and the menu items were named for the cross-country obstacles.

All of Canada was proud of the Olympic high flyers, and dedicated Canadian equestrians looked forward to the next set of games, where they might have their chance at Olympic glory.

Stables and Stars

What do a curvaceous movie star and a Canadian jumping horse have in common? In 1959, they both did their bit to promote the participation of a Canadian team in the Rome Olympics of 1960.

The horse was Roma, the big brown gelding designated to be Brian Herbinson's mount in Rome. The actress was Gina Lollobrigida, the alluring female lead of many a silver-screen epic. Ms. Lollobrigida, who was living in Toronto at the time, was asked if she would sponsor a new horse on the Canadian Olympic team, and she graciously obliged. Stacks of photos were taken of the athletic horse and beautiful actress, and newspaper editors everywhere ate the publicity stunt up. (It is not recorded anywhere how Roma felt about the media circus, nor if he was invited to attend the party Ms. Lollobrigida hosted for the team after the Olympics were over.)

Olympic Disaster

If you were to ask a cross-country competitor to describe the three-day event at the Rome Olympics of 1960 in one word, he or she would probably say "Disastrous!"

Brian Herbinson, Jim Elder, Norman Elder, and Tom Gayford were the riders faced with guiding, encouraging, and even babying the horses Roma, Canadian Envoy, Royal Beaver, and Pepper Knowes around the punishing course.

The altitude and heat combined to take a toll on riders and horses from every team that participated. Later on, Jim Elder said that the carnage among horses and riders during the cross-country phase of the Rome three-day event was "so appalling that authorities seriously considered removing future Three-Day Events from Olympic competitions." Although Elder also maintained that the jumps in Rome were not more difficult than those at Stockholm, he did say that, due to poor planning and construction, they were definitely more perilous. Solid timber had been used to construct the jumps in Sweden, but the obstacles on the course in Rome were composed of thin, easily broken tree trunks, sewer piping, and other less than stout material. In addition, the approaches to and landing areas after the jumps were sub-standard. This was proven when

Norman Elder and his mount fell at the second fence due to the sand on the landing side giving way.

The round endured by Pepper Knowes and Tom Gayford was a like a bad dream that keeps repeating and repeating. At a water obstacle, the horse fell and was completely covered by water. The only thing that saved him from drowning before help could arrive was Gayford's holding the horse's head above water. After the aquatic rescue, Gayford remounted and the pair carried on to the next jump, a woodpile, where the horse fell again. Somehow, a splinter of wood was driven into the horse's foot in such a way as to paralyse the injured leg. The Canadian team's veterinarian anesthetized the horse and removed the wood, with instantaneous results: the leg was sound again.

The horses were worn out by the mountainous terrain of the roads and tracks portion even before the cross-country phase started. The number of disqualified entrants ballooned upwards as horses and riders fell all over the course. Ambulances and even helicopters were needed in some of the rescues. Jim Elder described the area as being like a battlefield. Norman Elder happened upon one rider lying in the grass, having a heart attack. Gillian Wilson (owner of Pepper Knowes) was lunching in a tent with some friends. When she left, she found a horse lying dead outside.

Fortunately, neither the men nor the horses of the Canadian Olympic team suffered any lasting injury. Jim Elder and his mount, Canadian Envoy, were the only Canadian combination to finish the course, which garnered them an individual 10th place. However, the team was eliminated because other members were unable to finish.

"The presence of friends and members of their families didn't make up for the disappointments and frustrations," writes Zita Barbara May in her book *Canada's International Equestrians*. "It was generally agreed that 'Rome was a disaster'."

Perhaps the one good thing that came out of the Rome disaster was new and improved rules for designing cross-country courses.

Guts and Glory in Mexico

In 1968, after their high flyers sat out the previous Olympic Games, the people of Canada pinned their hopes on their "best of the best." They sent a show-jumping team to Mexico City, a team which included two men who had previously competed in Olympic three-day events: Jim Day on Canadian Club, Tom Gayford aboard Big Dee, and Jim Elder on The Immigrant. Terrance "Torchy" Millar and his mount, Beefeater, went to the games as a spare combination.

Captain Tom

Tom Gayford, stockbroker and avid horseman, had come by his love of riding honestly. He was the son of Colonel Gordon Gayford, an intense supporter of the Toronto and North York Hunt, who had also been a member of the Canadian team during international competitions.

Tom had accumulated an impressive array of honours, starting in the late 1940s when he began his riding career. A strong competitor, and a force to be reckoned with, Gayford and his mounts had posted numerous wins in both hunter and jumper events.

Gayford had been selected as part of the Canadian three-day event team for the 1956 Olympics, but decided he should stay at home because of business considerations. He continued to compete across North America in succeeding years in both show jumping and three-day events, and posted some of his most notable wins between 1956 and 1965, including three times winning the Puissance Wagstaff Challenge competition at the National Horse Show in New York with the incomparable Blue Beau.

When Gayford had the opportunity to attend the Mexico Olympics as part of the Canadian show-jumping team, he leapt at the chance and was chosen team captain.

Jim the Elder, Jim the Younger

Jim Elder's family farm north of Toronto was the scene of his first forays into the riding and jumping world. Elder joined the Canadian Equestrian Team in the 1950s, when he was chosen as a replacement after one of the team riders got sick. "Since they had some small horses left and I was a small guy, I got to go," Elder explained in a 1999 interview for CBC Sports Online.

Elder's self-depreciating comment made it sound like his participation with the team was a case of being in the right place at the right time, but in fact he possessed phenomenal riding ability. The talented horseman helped win a team bronze medal in the three-day event at the 1956 Stockholm Olympics, as well as numerous Pan-American Games medals. He competed regularly in both show jumping and three-day eventing.

Jim Day lived just the next farm over from Jim Elder and was an enthusiastic horseman from childhood. (His first mount was a little donkey named Buttermilk.) He often would ride across the back fields and jump the fence to get to Elder's farm, where the elder Jim would give riding advice to the younger Jim. Day's riding ability impressed Elder. "Jimmy Day was an exceptional rider," Elder continued in the same CBC interview. "He was like the Bobby Hull or Bobby Orr of jumping. He had talent oozing out."

Day began his equestrian career in 1964, when he was only 18 years of age. His performance at the International Junior Horse Show, held north of Toronto in Cedar Valley, earned him the title of North American Junior Jumping Champion, and he was selected for the Canadian show-jumping team.

Tough Timber

The jumping course in Mexico City was declared one of the toughest Olympic courses ever built, with 17 large fences set close together and at awkward angles. "They hired a Dutch course designer. They gave him the dimensions of the stadium and he designed it on paper," Elder later explained. "They neglected to tell him that at least 30 feet were needed on either side for the track and field. It shortened up the whole stadium, the whole ring. Instead of putting jumps where the designer wanted, they had to shorten them all, to smaller and different distances."

Team show jumping was the final event on the last day of the games. Germany, France, Great Britain, the United States, and Australia had all fielded strong teams. The Canadian team was relatively new, internationally, and the team riders were "virtually unknown," but at the start of the second round, they were close behind France in first place.

Hopes were high that the equestrian team could break the jinx that seemed to be plaguing Canadian athletes at these games. Up to this point, Canada had won only four medals in all disciplines, and there were no gold medals in the collection.

Big Dee, Big Mare for a Big Job

Team captain Gayford was the first Canadian to ride, on a mare called Big Dee, an also-ran from the racetrack, that became an Olympic star. Sired by Unsinatus, an imported grandson of Nearco, the 17 hh brown mare was bought as a four-year-old off the Fort Erie track by Tom Gayford and his father, Gordon, in 1963.

They paid a paltry $400 for her, and for the first year she was used as a mount in the Toronto and North York Hunt. Gordon Gayford found that although she could be careless over low jumps, Big Dee improved when put to large fences. It wasn't long before she said her last good-byes to the hunting field: Tom Gayford snapped her up as a hot Olympic prospect.

Prior to the games, Big Dee had distinguished herself by helping the Canadian team win a bronze medal in the show-jumping competition at the 1967 Pan-American Games in Winnipeg. With this accolade under her girth, Gayford set his sights on higher aspirations and felt that Big Dee was a mare who could do the job.

At the '68 Olympics, she proved that she could.

"I had a little more experience, and once I got around [the course], I could come back and say, 'Okay, watch that corner down there, it's tough getting into that combination, and the time is tight'," explained Gayford in a 1999 interview for *The Olympians*, found at CBC-TV Online. "I went in there and the next guy knew exactly what to do and where I lost it."

Canadian Club

The next Canadian team member to ride was Jim Day, on Canadian Club. Another horse bought off the track, the chestnut Thoroughbred, standing 16.3 hh, became an exceptional jumper and went on to record impressive wins throughout his career. He attacked jumping courses with bravery, power, and boldness.

He began his career in Florida in 1966, claiming the title of Champion of the Circuit. In Harrisburg, Pennsylvania, on the fall circuit, he jumped six feet nine inches, and later, at the National Horse Show in New York, he flew over the bar at seven feet one inch.

In the year prior to the Olympics, Canadian Club and Jim Day competed in the Winnipeg Pan-Am Games, on the same team as Gayford and Elder. This spring-loaded horse earned an individual gold medal for jumping. He leaped a height of seven feet three inches, setting a Puissance record in the process. He was deemed to be one of the greatest Canadian-bred horses of the era.

Canadian Club thrived on competition, and in Mexico he gave Day an excellent ride, posting only 12 faults. This turned up the heat on the French team's final rider. If he posted a good round, Canada's hopes for a gold would be dashed. But the Canadian team still had its "ace in the hole" with Jim Elder and The Immigrant.

The Immigrant, Olympic Rodeo Star

All horse enthusiasts, whether they own their own equines or simply love them from afar, have a favourite. Sometimes a horse is loved for his ability, sometimes for a facet of his character, such as his attitude or simply because he returns the love lavished on him by his owner.

The Immigrant was a horse with an incredible jumping capability, which garnered him many fans. But what really seemed to grab people was his propensity for misbehaviour under saddle. The talented high flyer couldn't keep his feet on the ground, even between the jumps. It was nothing for him to flourish his heels in the air after a jump, making the job of piloting him akin to riding a bucking bronco at the Calgary Stampede. It is amazing that a horse with such unorthodox style turned into an Olympic star.

Bob Ballard originally bought The Immigrant from a member of the Ox Ridge Hunt in Darien, Connecticut. Ballard then turned around and sold the horse to former Olympic skater Bill McLachlan as a prospect for the show-jumping circuit. Knowing that McLachlan didn't plan to ride the horse himself, Ballard suggested that Jim Elder might be interested in taking the mount. (Many riders don't own their own horses, but instead ride animals owned by people who love horses and jumping competitions and want to take part in the excitement of showing, but who don't ride themselves, or have bought the horse as an investment. These people buy horses and donate them for use by the Canadian team.)

In 1968, The Immigrant was still a young horse, and crowds sometimes excited him. He got plenty of excitement at the Olympics. It took all of Elder's skill to maintain the equilibrium of both his horse and himself. "When you're standing there and coming down the ramp and the crowd, the feeling of the crowd in the big Olympic stadium, it's really quite a feeling," recalled Elder for the CBC *Olympians* interview. "The horse feels it too, you could just feel his heart. It was pounding about a hundred miles an hour."

The last rider for the French team went just before Elder. Unfortunately, the stress of competition got to both the Frenchman and his mount, and their final score was a whopping 28 faults. Suddenly Canada was back in the chase for the gold, and it all hinged on Jim Elder and The Immigrant.

Horse and rider bounded over the first six obstacles and left them standing. So far, so good. But at the seventh obstacle, The Immigrant's leg brushed a rail, and down it went. With intense concentration and skill — and a good dose of luck — the pair was able to finish the course with no other faults. Final score: Canada, 102.75 faults; France, 110.50 faults; and Germany, 117.25 faults.

Won By a Whisker

When all the horses had completed the course and the points were tallied, the Canadians had won the gold medal by the slimmest of margins — a mere 7.75 faults. The jubilant team members performed their victory gallop before packed stands. The glow of their accomplishment was rivalled only by the shine of Canada's first and only gold medal of the Mexico Olympics.

The members of the 1968 Olympic team surmounted a string of obstacles, both in getting to the prestigious event and at the event itself. They pulled off one of the most exciting upset wins in Olympic history.

Chapter 4
Barra Lad: Four-Legged Dynamite

P art Hackney, part Standardbred. One breed known for its high-stepping, showy gait; the other for its speed on the racetrack. Not, by any stretch of the imagination, a cross that any knowledgeable horseman would purposely choose in an effort to breed a prospective jumping horse. But in Barra Lad's case, it resulted in one of the most spectacular high-flying jumping horses of all time. He was like four-legged dynamite, exploding over jumps.

The Horse
Essondale, near Coquitlam, British Columbia, was the

location of Colony Farm, an experimental farm facility that gained international recognition for breeding top-quality Holstein cows. It seems incongruous that a strangely bred foal like Barra Lad ended up there, but he was simply the result of a "Hey, baby, I've jumped the fence and no one's looking" unplanned liaison between his Hackney father and Standardbred-type mother. In any event, Barra Lad was born in 1918, and since his dam died shortly after his birth, he required human intervention and bottle-feeding to survive.

As orphan foals are prone to do, he became more than a little spoiled. Naturally, he viewed his human nursemaids as surrogate mothers, and as he was so friendly, he quickly became a favourite of the farm workers.

It is easy to picture him in the mind's eye: impossibly long-legged and awkward, with a fuzzy foal face, and that whisk-broom tail flapping like a windshield wiper as he prances about the farm, poking his white-blazed muzzle into places it doesn't belong and generally making a nuisance of himself. Oh, see him now! There he is, over at the clothesline. Look at that little imp, his bright, intelligent eyes dancing with mischief as he grabs a freshly washed bedsheet in his teeth. He tugs at it until, snip-snap, the clothespins zing free and away he races, the sheet billowing about his ears and trailing out behind him like an oversized, tailless kite.

Unfortunately, cute tricks can quickly turn into annoying habits, and the little orphan prince's freedom to roam the farm was curtailed shortly after his escapades became too much to endure. Time passed and he grew into a sterling example of teenage horsehood. The fuzzy colt became a strapping bay horse, solid of muscle, shiny of coat, with unblemished confirmation, keen intelligence, and a captivating disposition.

As the young prince grew, he began to show a predisposition to jump whatever got in his way. He would much rather go *over* obstacles in his path than go around them. It was not unusual for Bill McVee, the farm superintendent, to visit the colt's paddock only to find that the impudent upstart had pulled a Harry Houdini act, escaped the confines of his corral, and was unconcernedly grazing where the grass was always greener.

Naturally, the fences were built higher after each breakout, but their efforts to contain the rascal were fruitless; no matter how high the fences were built, he jumped over them.

The Man
While the orphan colt was growing up in BC, the man who would play an important part in his destiny was

establishing himself 700 kilometres away in Calgary. That man was Peter Welsh.

Welsh was a Scotsman who had emigrated from the Old Country in the early 1900s. A canny soul, he had numerous children and even more numerous business ideas. Little information can be found about Welsh before he left his homeland; however, his coups in Canada are countless.

Welsh set about building an empire in his new home. One of its most notable elements was the Calgary Sales Repository, among the first livery stables in the city of Calgary. His success was due in large part to the fact that Welsh had a keen eye for a horse and was known as one of the finest judges of horseflesh in Canada in his time. The Canadian Pacific Railway hired him to buy horses for settlers coming to new farms under CPR's land settlement plan. This gave Welsh the opportunity to search for fine horses for himself as well, and he gained a reputation as quite a horse trader. Horses were his business, but high jumpers were his passion. He set his sights on having a stable full of the best high-jumping horses and went about accomplishing that goal.

Welsh had seven children — Alphie, Cathy, John, Josie, Mary, Louis, and Peter. Most of them were given riding lessons practically before they could walk, although Mary was terrified of horses and never rode. Their ambitious father soon had them competing in horse shows. He became a trophy hunter, and as the children racked up more and more wins, they also developed a string of talented jumping horses second to none.

Welsh's stable of high-flying horses and fearless young riders became renowned throughout the horse-show circuit. Crowds flocked to see their performances. Horse shows were notorious for running late into the night; nevertheless, loyal fans waited sometimes as late as 3:00 am to watch the Welsh children display their prowess. Little Alphie Welsh was an especial favourite, piloting an elegant, dock-tailed grey mare called Mademoiselle.

Once Welsh achieved his dream of owning the best horses in Canada, he immediately pressed on towards another goal, seeking even higher acclaim: he wanted to own a world champion high jumper.

The Partnership

Horsemen like to brag about their horses. So, in the spring of 1921, when Bill McVee mentioned to Welsh that there was a colt at home in BC that could jump out of any field they put him in, Welsh lost no time in deciding to buy the horse. He offered $150 (equivalent to about $1300 today) without even seeing the animal. What faith! What optimism! What a fortuitous deal for Welsh.

When the young prince arrived at his new home, he was given the official show name Barra Lad, in honour of Mrs. Welsh's Scottish birthplace. He was stabled with Mademoiselle, and the two animals became fast friends. They were so close that it seemed as if Barra Lad, the orphan foal, had found a new mother, and Mademoiselle had found a new child. They disliked being separated from each other, and during Barra Lad's future jumping competitions, the grey mare had to be brought into the ring in order to calm him down.

Barra Lad was put into training with Louis and Josie Welsh, Peter's two eldest sons. It was between the Lad and Louis that a special rapport developed. Louis had the gift of "horseman's hands" — quiet, kind, guiding, and supportive. Barra Lad responded to Louis with the gifts that great horses give their riders: affection and a willingness to give their all.

Under the boys' tutelage, the Lad blossomed, his abilities increased, and Peter Welsh decided to take the three-year-old wonder horse east to test his mettle and see how he stacked up against the "big names" in the show ring of the day. When he began triumphing over experienced veterans of jumping competitions from the

Atlantic to the Pacific, the Welsh family horsemen discovered they had a real champion in their possession.

The Challenge

Imagine how it would feel to try and jump over an obstacle that is higher than you are tall. You can't see what's on the other side, so it's a jump into the unknown, pure and simple — equivalent to closing your eyes and walking off the edge of a cliff.

Horses chasing the high-jump record face this challenge repeatedly. Yet, time after time, they thunder powerfully towards a jump and propel themselves into the air ... up, up, up! ... in an effort to clear the opponent obstacle. To fail means disqualification at best, serious injury at worst. But Barra Lad met the challenge over and over again.

Following his success with the Calgary Sales Repository, Peter Welsh had yet another brain wave: Why not start a travelling rodeo show? And so, the Alberta Stampede Company was born, with Welsh's stable of high jumpers as the main attraction in addition to the rodeo acts on the bill.

People were fascinated by Barra Lad's jumping prowess and eccentric disposition. Gentle and friendly to work around in his stall, he was the epitome of an ideal mount. Who could ever imagine that this mellow

Barra Lad: Four-Legged Dynamite

Louis Welsh, aged 15, jumping Barra Lad in 1923.

creature, ambling down the side of a sun-dappled country road on a fine summer day, as meek and gentle as an old stable hack for hire, had an aberration? But he had the equine equivalent of a Jekyll-and-Hyde personality. As soon as a rider brought him into the show ring and pointed him at a jump, Barra Lad turned into a snorting, fire-breathing monster.

"It's hard to explain," Louis Welsh said in an interview in the Summer 1977 edition of *Golden West* magazine. "He could be so gentle and quiet, but when he got in the ring he got so excited we couldn't hold him. I've seen two men try to hold him and two men try to get me on top. He'd kick and bite, but I wasn't afraid of him."

Higher and Higher

In 1922, at the Brandon Spring Show, Barra Lad wowed the crowd by establishing a Manitoba record when he leaped over the bars set at 6 feet 10 inches on the Monday night of the show. Only three days later, he blasted his own previous record off the books, surpassing it by an amazing three inches when he cleared the height of seven feet one inch.

Between 1922 and 1925, Barra Lad's amazing leaps continued to dominate the high-jump statistics. For seven consecutive days, he performed and cleared the seven-foot mark at a huge show in Seattle, Washington. Following his triumphs in Seattle, the Lad was taken back home to Calgary, where, on April 1, 1925, he played to the home crowd with gusto for the final time, jumping a bar set at seven feet one inch. Scarcely six months later, Barra Lad reached the pinnacle of his career, not at home in Calgary, but in New Westminster, BC.

The great horse's fame was such that, on the night of his record-breaking jump, the host arena — designed to hold 6000 people — was bursting at the seams. Spectators streamed in, ticket sellers were kept on the hop, and the building's balconies, one above the other, were in danger of collapsing from the weight of all the eager high-jump aficionados. The building inspector and fire marshal were trying to stop ticket sales and eject a number of the people who were already in the stands, but others kept piling in.

On this auspicious occasion, the official measuring was being done by two Supreme Court judges. Fred Kennedy, a newspaper reporter and Welsh's publicity director, was in the ring as well. Josie and Fred Welsh were in position at either side of the obstacle. If horse or rider got into trouble, it was their job to release the top bars. (Archival photographs of Barra Lad and other horses in high-jump competitions show a jumping structure shaped like a flat-bottomed U. The sides of the U form an alleyway, which the horse enters on his way to the obstacle. The jump itself consists of a number of poles parallel to the ground; in some of the photos, the upper poles are tied or held onto the corner uprights, which are set into the ground. In others, the parallel poles are only on the upper half of the jump; the lower half is piled with what appears to be cut brush.)

Although Barra Lad had come into the arena with an uncharacteristically quiet demeanour, when he began to pick up the frenzied vibes of the swelling crowd, he started getting excited himself.

He warmed up by frisking over a jump set at six feet. The bars were raised, and he then faced up to the seven-foot jump, floating over as lightly as thistledown drifts on a summer breeze. At that point, Fred Kennedy made an announcement that silenced the crowd: the champion would attempt to clear 8 feet 1.5 inches and set a world high-jumping record.

Everyone was focussed on Barra Lad and his youthful rider as they walked up to the jump and stood there looking at it. "Usually I'd never do that with him," Louis said in an interview years later, "because he'd have gone right through it."

Just as carefully, Louis guided his horse back to the starting point. Then he turned Barra Lad around and the horse accelerated towards the jump. At the last minute, without warning, the Lad stopped dead and ducked sideways, bumping some of the lower poles, which were loosely stacked on the jump. Louis yelled at the attendants and judges to hurry and get the poles back in place: he could feel his horse reaching the point of no return — he was ready to give the jump a try.

Again Louis took the champion back to the end of the ring. The starter waved the flag, and, responding to the urging of his rider's hands and voice, the exuberant horse raced towards the jump, with Louis flattened low over his neck.

With seemingly effortless strides, Barra Lad bore down on the obstacle and then, at its very base, he sprang powerfully off his haunches and bounded into the air, as a partridge flushed by a hunter bursts out of the brush to freedom in the sky.

Time slowed and seemed to stop as he cleaved the air on his way to the summit of the jump. Such was the power and scope of his leap that his front legs cleared the bar by a good six inches; however, his hindquarters were trailing out behind him, and he looked to be in danger of knocking the whole obstacle down. At the last second, the valiant warrior tucked his hind legs up, too, and in an instant, with almost unbelievable power, surged over the top and descended the other side.

The force of his trajectory was so great that he was unable to land normally on his front feet. Instead, he stumbled to his knees. Because his neck was still outstretched, his muzzle dug a large groove in the dirt of the arena floor. He scrambled to his feet amid exultant cheers and thunderous applause. He had done it! Barra Lad, a true Canadian hero, had set a world record with a mark of 8 feet 1.5 inches.

The crowd went wild, swarming down into the ring and surrounding the champion, eager to pat him and congratulate his rider. In the same manner that the Kentucky Derby winner is awarded a wreath of flowers, Barra Lad's neck was adorned with a floral horseshoe, and the riotous strains of "There'll Be a Hot Time in the Old Town Tonight" blared through the building as the band swung into action.

There was such a crush that police were required to control the crowd so the hero could be returned to the barn. After he was cooled down, Barra Lad was tucked up in his stall and given his feed.

The Aftermath

Long into the night, Peter Welsh, his family, and cohorts discussed Barra Lad's future. Ideas for new records to attempt flew fast and furious. There was even a Hollywood movie to be made. Finally, the Welshes retired for a few hours of sleep. An early morning loomed, as the whole shebang — riders and horses — was due at the county fair in Puyallup, Washington. But morning began even earlier than anticipated.

Peter Welsh was jerked from slumber by the strident ring of the phone. The call summoned him to the barn: Barra Lad was sick! Welsh woke Kennedy, and they lost no time in getting to the stable, where groom Pat Young gave them sombre news. Barra Lad, usually eager for his mash, hadn't touched it. Even worse, he had suddenly lowered his head, falling face first into a corner of the stall, injuring himself above the eyes.

Doctors Agar and Black, government veterinarians, got the horse up and into the barn alleyway and commenced working on him. By this time, Barra Lad was bleeding from the mouth; the vets suspected internal hemorrhaging.

The vets worked feverishly as, all around them, preparations were being made to load horses, tack, and equipment on the train nearby. One by one the horses were led away. The last to go was Barra Lad's closest companion, the grey mare Mademoiselle. She had become increasingly upset as the drama unfolded and was reluctant to leave her stricken stablemate, but finally, after stopping to gently nose him and nicker, she too was led away.

Shortly thereafter, with none of the fanfare that heralded his life, Barra Lad quietly died.

The Record That Wasn't

The scene of Barra Lad's greatest triumph became that of his greatest tragedy. He was buried on the grounds of the arena, with his horseshoe victory wreath, by now withered, the only marker of his final resting place.

The autopsy done after Barra Lad died showed that the main artery leading to his liver had been ruptured, resulting in the hemorrhage. Louis Welsh thought that the shock of the jump and landing was to blame. "It's too high for any horse; they can't reach the ground," he told the interviewer from *Golden West* magazine in 1977. "You know it's foolishness when you start jumping like that. It's crazy."

Sadly, that world record jump was never recognized by the *Guinness Book of Records*. In fact, Barra Lad's name is not mentioned in that tome at all. The Welsh family was so overwhelmed by the unexpectedness of Barra Lad's tragic death that no one gave a thought to notifying the authorities at Guinness of the new record. Captain A. Larraguibel Morales and his mount, Huasó, are listed as the official high-jump champions, with a record of 2.47 metres (8 feet 1.25 inches) in Santiago, Chile, on February 5, 1949.

Today, no statue marks the burial site of Canada's greatest jumping horse. The arena in which he set the record was destroyed by fire over 30 years ago. Aside from a handful of photographs in the Glenbow Foundation archives, a few magazine articles, and a chapter in Grant MacEwan's book *Memory Meadows*, Barra Lad has been almost forgotten.

But in the imagination of those who aspire to surpass his record, he lives on: one of the greatest high flyers of them all.

Chapter 5
Equine Quirks

ny horseman worth his or her oats will tell you that, like humans, no two horses are exactly the same. When put to work, a properly trained horse will, for the most part, always do his best to accomplish the task you've asked of him. Horsemen have a term for this trait: they call it "honesty."

However, a horse can be as honest as the day is long and still have idiosyncrasies. Perhaps a draft horse works better if he is harnessed on the right side of the team harness, rather than the left. Perhaps the racing Thoroughbred will refuse to be led into the horse trailer, but will walk in quietly by himself, with the end of the lead shank merely thrown over his withers. There are probably as many different equine quirks as there are different equines!

The horses in this chapter were all high-flying stars in their own right, but in addition, they all had unusual eccentricities that added excitement to the lives of their owners and fans.

Montreal, The Reluctant Competitor

Canadian equestrians have a long history of competing — and winning — at Madison Square Gardens in New York City. The November 12, 1929, issue of the *Toronto Mail and Empire* featured a photo of Lieutenant C.C. Mann and his mount Montreal. The pair had won the trophy for the international military stake at the Gardens, besting 30 other riders from five countries.

The majority of show-jumping horses are eager to compete in the show ring. While Montreal was an excellent jumping horse, what made him noteworthy was not his ability as a high flyer, but rather his reticence about entering the ring at this particular show. He was so unenthusiastic that it was laughable.

According to Zita Barbara May, Lieutenant Mann and Montreal were waiting their turn at ringside. Mann prepared to mount just as the announcer heralded their arrival in the ring. The announcement startled Montreal and he jerked back, snapped a rein, and broke free. He decamped at high speed, back to his stall; Lieutenant Mann was ingloriously left behind on the ground.

The National Horse Show had used and appreciated the expert announcing services of Otis Trowbridge for a number of years, and he and his audiences enjoyed a longstanding camaraderie. Trowbridge apparently decided to milk this disappearing horse act for all it was worth.

While another competitor rode in Lieutenant Mann's place, Trowbridge, with counterfeit consternation, apologized for his "mistake." Montreal was fetched back to ringside, wearing a new, strong bridle that the harried grooms had found and hastily substituted for the broken one.

Trowbridge again announced, "Lieutenant C.C. Mann on Montreal," having seen them appear at ringside to await their chance to compete. It was déjà vu. The announcement was accompanied by the sound of reverberating hoofbeats. Montreal again fled, this time leaving his whole bridle behind as he sought the safety of his home away from home. In mock sorrow, Trowbridge broadcast to the crowd that he had gotten it wrong again and introduced another rider instead.

The Canadian team's aggravated officials deserved full points for perseverance. The groom, with the recalcitrant Montreal in tow, was directed to lead the horse into the ring and allow Mann to mount the horse inside the gate.

These antics caused the announcer to pretend that he was mightily embarrassed by his previous announcing errors. "Ladies and gentlemen," Trowbridge shouted, "I crave your forgiveness ... called it wrong again! Lieutenant C.C. Mann, Canada, *with* Montreal!"

At this point, Lieutenant Mann's groom, discomfited by the circus-like events, gave the rider such a powerful boost up into the saddle that Mann's momentum carried him right over Montreal's back and down onto the arena floor again. The building resounded with chortles and guffaws.

Mann finally succeeded in mounting the bashful Montreal, and the horse sprang over the jumps with enough skill and panache to win the $1000 Military Jumping Stake.

Poor Montreal. How ironic that the jumping star should be so introverted when he shared a name with Montreal, a city known for its extroverted inhabitants.

Michael, Horse of Iron

Just imagine the consternation and outrage that would erupt today among show-jumping competitors if they were asked to go back into the ring and repeat their jumping round, over and over and over!

Modern competitions commonly consist of two rounds, followed by a jump-off to break any ties. However, prior to 1949, when the "one jump-off, fewest faults, fastest time" method of determining winners was adopted, Canadian show-jumping competitions involved multiple jump-offs. The horses kept going round the whole course until one emerged with the fewest — or no — faults. Quite naturally, horses with the strongest constitution and in the best condition usually captured the prize.

Michael had been purchased in the early 1920s by Colonel R.S. McLaughlin of Oshawa, Ontario, who wanted a mannerly horse for his own use. McLaughlin ordered his daughter Eleanor not to touch the horse, but she sneaked him out of the stable to test his jumping ability — which she found to be terrific.

When he found out about this direct violation of his edict, her father was incensed, but when he calmed down, he made Eleanor a gift of Michael. The young lady and her horse began entering — and winning — horse shows, which set the stage for Michael's appearance with C.C. Mann (Eleanor's husband) at the Royal of 1932.

In the first go-round, Michael and 31 other horses navigated the prescribed course, which included a gate (set at four feet six inches), a stone gate (four feet eight inches), and a triple jump (three elements ranging from 4 feet 10 inches to five feet two inches). Nine of the horses had no faults.

The second round of jumping pared that number down to four. By the fifth jump-off there were only two competitors in the running: Roxana and Michael.

A jump-off is an arduous experience for any horse. To be included, they've already gone around the course twice, with no faults. Make no mistake, by the end of the second round, most horse are tired! The jump-off, in which they must again go clean, as well as faster than any other horse in order to win, can be exhausting. So just imagine how these final two competitors felt, as each entered the ring for the fifth time ...

Roxana went first and sailed around the course perfectly — until the last jump, where she bumped a top rail off. Michael alone was left in the running. Could he do it?

He did! The horse with the seemingly iron constitution whisked around the course one last time, leaving every obstacle standing and posting yet another clear round. He had cleared 40 jumps since the start of the class and more than deserved the silver trophy he won.

Roger II, From Buggy to Bounder

If the brown gelding named Roger II had been more amenable and not earned a reputation as a rogue in harness, he might never have found his true calling and won the prestigious President of Mexico's Trophy at the Royal Winter Fair Horse Show in 1949.

In that competition, for the first time, the Royal adopted the standardized rules of the Fédération Equestre Internationale (International Equestrian Federation). Up until then, the Royal — and other Canadian horse shows — scored jumping competitions by using "slats" — thin slips of wood placed along the tops of jumps, which, when dislodged, counted as faults against the horse.

These slats caused enormous kerfuffle at shows. A horse received four faults if he knocked slats off with his front legs, but only two faults if he hit them with his hind. This made score-keeping a nightmare for the officials, as they had to decide if the slats had been disturbed when the horse was going up or coming down. As well, there was no time limit to the classes; rather, jump-offs were used to determine a winner in the event of a tie score. If there were several good jumpers in a class, the jump-offs just kept going on and on, sometimes all night.

By 1949, 37 countries had adopted the FEI rules,

which used the "least amount of faults in the fastest time" method. FEI officials were receiving complaints from international team riders about the Canadian show rules, and they soon dictated that international teams would no longer compete at the Royal if the show did not join the FEI. Despite objections (in some cases quite vehement) from Canadian officials and riders alike, the Canadian Horse Shows Association adopted the FEI rules, but the Royal Winter Fair refused.

However, the Royal did schedule a special jumping competition on the last night of the 1949 fair, which would use the FEI rules. It was also the first time in Canada that members of international military teams and civilians competed together. The President of Mexico donated a trophy for the winner.

Fifteen extremely colourful jumps were set up in the ring, to the horror of a number of horses that balked at going over them. The rainbow-coloured obstacles didn't faze Roger II — he was game to jump anything. He loved to jump!

A Mennonite farmer in Hamburg, Ontario, had acquired the bounding bay gelding as a showy candidate to pull his buggy to church, but Roger had higher aspirations than being a harness horse. All the other horses stood patiently, quietly waiting until the service was over. Not Roger. He got bored, kicked the buggy into firewood, shucked off his bridle, nonchalantly scaled the fence, and lit out for the comforts of home. He also had a propensity for escaping from the pasture, clearing the five-foot-high boundary fence in the process.

Judge G.A. Brickenden, who owned a line of exceptional jumping horses, was alerted to Roger's existence by a friend. Brickenden lost no time in going to see if this horse could be bought and brought into his stable, driving up to Hamburg on a Sunday afternoon.

Brickenden found Roger to be mannerly and sound of wind and limb. The farmer promised that Roger had none of the usual equine vices; his only fault was his love of jumping — a deplorable flaw, in the farmer's opinion. Trying not to appear overly eager, Judge Brickenden offered to buy Roger on the spot and take his chances with the hopping hoodlum.

The farmer would not compromise his religious beliefs by making a Sunday deal, no matter how eager he was to part company with the unsuitable equine. He refused to take payment that day, but told Brickenden to come back the following day with $250 and a horse trailer. Not surprisingly, Brickenden did.

He had got the deal of the decade. Roger moved into the Brickenden Stables and became a champion jumping horse — and the one who won the President of Mexico's special trophy. Pretty good, for a buggy horse.

Chapter 6
Big Ben: From Commoner to King

There have been thousands of good jumping horses in Canada, and hundreds of excellent ones. A few dozen were exceptional. But once in a very great while a horse comes along that is extraordinary, one that outshines all the others, the brightest star blazing in the show-jumping sky. Big Ben was such a horse.

He wasn't particularly pretty. Those in the know thought he was too big and awkward to handle the tight turns and corners of a show-jumping ring. And he made a peculiar "un-h, un-h" noise in his throat when he galloped.

A number of professional horsemen passed him up

as a jumping prospect. Then Ian Millar heard about him, saw him, tried him, bought him — and the pair started climbing the ladder to success, reaching for that elusive prize found at the upper echelons of show jumping.

The Early Years

He was born in 1976 on the farm of Jacobus van Hooydonk and Louisa van Looveren in Wuustweezel (Woost-*way*-zl), near Antwerp, Belgium. He was by the stallion Etretat (*Ate*-ra-tah), and out of the good mare Ookie (*Oo*-key). By some ever-interesting quirk of genetics, the traits of the 16 hh stallion combined with those of the 15.3 hh mare to produce a large liver chestnut colt who would grow into a 17.3 hh colossus. (By way of comparison, consider that the standard height for a door in your home is 80 inches — so if Big Ben stood in a doorway, you could only get a sheet of typing paper, lying on its long edge, between his withers and the top edge of the door. That's a *really* big horse.)

The rules of the Belgian Warmblood society dictate that, each year, all foals born of registered parents must have names starting with a particular letter. In 1976, foals' names had to start with "w." Van Hooydonk admired Winston Churchill, so he christened the gangly foal Winston.

After an uneventful colthood, van Hooydonk

turned the one-and-a-half-year-old Winston out to pasture for the summer to grow and mature. With only his younger sister and the wild birds for company, Winston ate, slept, and whiled away his "teenage" period, perfectly content to be a loner.

When he was brought in for the winter, it took an effort to get past his natural reserve and shyness. Van Hooydonk and his family used friendly persuasion — and a special treat of sugar — to curry favour with the four-legged recluse. Winston was again turned out the following spring for another season of R and R. But it was when he was reintroduced to the barn routine the next winter that he began to show his true colours.

The Unnatural Natural

Calling someone or something a freak may be a putdown in any other context, but on the Grand Prix showjumping circuit, a rider with a "freak" horse is someone to be envied. Most horses don't have a natural inclination to jump over obstacles, and those that *can* jump well have usually received hours upon hours of training. But all the training in the world means nothing if the horse doesn't have the courage, natural aptitude, and deep reserve of power required to jump huge fences again and again and again. Riders search long and hard, trying to find just such a special horse.

Like most horsemen, Jacobus van Hooydonk cared about his horses. To keep Winston from being bored, and as a suppling exercise, Jacobus began giving the horse some freedom in the indoor ring. And that's where Winston's unnatural natural traits came to light.

There was a jump set up in the ring, and Winston — under no restraint or guidance, and with no urging from anyone — started jumping it, all by himself. Jacobus was astounded: in all his years of horse breeding and raising, he had never seen anything like it. To his knowledge, Winston had never jumped anything before, and yet here he was, jumping this obstacle repeatedly, three times in a row.

When put into training under saddle, Winston proved to be as fastidious about where he placed his feet and body as he was in choosing his friends. Daniel van Hooydonk, Jacobus's son, began riding Winston in horse shows and found an eager competitor under his saddle. The horse was so enthralled with jumping that he jumped "big" — leaping much higher than the jump required, leaving lots of space between himself and the obstacle.

In the summer of 1983, Winston took first place in two of the four dressage competitions in which Daniel entered him and posted three clear rounds in four show-jumping events. Winston was now seven years old, and his life of relative obscurity was about to end.

A Rose By Any Other Name

Later in 1983, horse trainer and rider Bert Romp arrived from Tilburg, Holland, a short distance from Wuustweezel. He was in Belgium looking for likely jumper prospects, and he happened to look at the big gelding belonging to the van Hooydonks. Romp was not overly impressed with Winston's conformation, deriding his short neck, big head, and skinny appearance, but Jacobus earnestly recounted all of Winston's good qualities to Romp. When the dealing was done, Romp had purchased the tall horse for 100,000 Belgian francs (about $2000).

Romp moved Winston to his farm in Holland and put him into training. The man was exasperated by Winston's less-than-brave demeanour — the horse was a titan in size, but timorous in manner. He was afraid of many things, even something as innocuous as water. But he could certainly jump great heights.

Mrs. Romp was responsible for giving Winston the nickname by which he became famous — Big Ben — because she thought he was as tall as the London tower that houses the famous clock. Bert Romp entered Big Ben in some jumping events in Holland, but did not have stellar results. Sometimes Ben would clear the huge fences, sometimes not.

Other horsemen, on the lookout for a winner, came to Romp's farm to see Ben, but they were as unimpressed by him as Romp was. The most desirable traits for a winning jumping horse are power, speed, bravery, and manoeuvrability, like a racy sports car, and ideally, the animal should be about 16 hh.

Ben seemed to be the complete opposite of this ideal — he was more like a Mack truck than a racy sports car. Those knowledgeable horsemen, no doubt employing logic and hard-won experience in their decisions, were understandably afraid that his huge size would be a detriment to his athleticism. They concluded he wouldn't be as fast and nimble as a smaller horse. And so they all passed him by as a potential winning mount.

Crossing Paths

The people involved in Grand Prix jumping, like those in most niche sports, make up a small and close-knit society. It is not unusual for participants to know most of the other athletes competing in the sport.

Emile Hendrix rode on the Dutch national team, Ian Millar on the Canadian one. Millar admired Hendrix's ability to assess the needs of riders in relation to their riding styles (European and North American styles *do* differ), to gauge the dollar value of a particular horse on both sides of the Atlantic, and to match the best horse and rider. Millar considered Hendrix "clever, an ethical horseman, a brilliant culler of horses," and "one of the best horse dealers in the world." So when Hendrix talked, Millar listened.

Spruce Meadows, High-Flying Horse Heaven

When most people looked at the site of a former cattle feedlot outside Calgary in the early 1970s, they saw, well, a cattle feedlot. Ron and Marg Southern saw into the future and envisioned a multi-purpose horse-show facility. That vision evolved into the ultimate horse lover's heaven, Spruce Meadows, which in 2002 was ranked Number One in the world.

This Canadian crown jewel of horse complexes is home to between 80 and 100 horses all year, but that number increases to 700 or more during major events like the Spruce Meadows Masters or North American tournament. This influx of equines is housed in the 400 temporary and 300 permanent stalls.

Spruce Meadows hosts four major outdoor tournaments throughout the year, held in six different outdoor show rings, and these prestigious events — not to mention the generous prize money available — have drawn national, Olympic, European, and world champion show jumpers, all eager to strut their stuff at Spruce.

Competitions at Spruce Meadows feature some of
the finest equestrian athletes in the world.

The Spruce Meadows International Show Ring is a
picture. Jewel-green grass sets off the handsome clock-
tower entrance to the ring and the challenging jumps.
The dreaded devil's dyke is one obstacle that has
claimed many an otherwise clear round. The competitors must jump over a rail into this rectangular-shaped
corral, go down an incline to another jump over water,
then up a hill and jump back out.

With over 100 grooms, trainers, and maintenance

and administration personnel, both full-time and part-time, and over 500 volunteer workers in the summer, Spruce Meadows is a veritable beehive of activity from sun up till sun down, year round. Since the first tournament held in 1976, when approximately 12 spectators walked through the gates, this superb venue has welcomed ever-swelling crowds of show-jumping fans. The Masters Tournament held on September 8, 2002, broke all previous attendance records and posted a new high of 57,222 spectators.

It was at Spruce Meadows, in late September 1983, where Hendrix and Millar first spoke about Big Ben. Millar was headed to Belgium, and Hendrix invited him to visit while in Europe. Millar went to Brussels, completed his business, and gave Hendrix a call. The horseman, acting as an agent for Bert Romp, told Millar there was a horse he should view, stabled about an hour away from Brussels. Millar recounted this particular conversation with Hendrix, and the horse dealer's ambivalence about Big Ben, in his autobiography, *Riding High: Ian Millar's World of Show Jumping*.

"I don't know whether you'd like him or not," Millar quoted Hendrix in one chapter. "He's a great big horse. You might really hate him, and it might be a total waste of time, but there's a chance that you might find it interesting, too."

As Millar prepared to go and see the horse, he was sceptical. He concluded, logically enough, that if other expert horsemen had rejected the horse as a prospective Grand Prix contender because of his size and looks, then maybe there was something wrong with the animal. "The horse was seven years old by this time and still nobody was buying him," Millar recalled in his book. "Such a situation always makes me nervous. If my peers are saying 'no', then maybe I should listen to them.

"Everybody felt the same. They looked at this somewhat bad-tempered horse, a big monster of a thing, not the best looking, and what they really saw was the proverbial bull in a china shop. He could jump, but would he ever fit into today's indoor show rings, or handle the course? Could he be a modern-day show jumper? If he was not too clumsy, would he be able to shorten his stride? Given his size, would he be fast enough?"

However, as soon as Millar saw Big Ben, something clicked, and as a result, Millar's evaluation of the horse flew in the face of all his standard horse-buying practices. Where he normally would let a dealer present the horse to him — a process that can take over 15 minutes — Millar instead began directing Bert Romp to show him Ben's different gaits and the level of his athleticism by doing a flying lead change and trotting over a jump.

Millar said he loved Ben's trot, describing it as "loose, easy, powerful."

Everything Millar had seen about Ben thus far was pleasing to him. In another departure from normal routine, Ian asked almost immediately to ride the big horse. "For some reason I escalated the process this time," Millar explained. "Everything was telling me, 'I love this horse'."

Millar went with his instincts and made a deal for the giant horse with the attitude, paying Bert Romp $45,000 — considerably more than Bert had paid for the horse only six weeks previously. And so the big, ugly horse from Belgium with the British-sounding name made the trip to his new home in Canada, leaving his life as an equine commoner behind.

Prince in Training

Settling into the routine at Millar Brooke Farm in Perth, Ontario, Big Ben became a prince in training. As Millar started riding him regularly, he became familiar with the horse's unconventional characteristics and extraordinary abilities. He also began to figure out how to work with Ben to harness those characteristics and abilities in the show ring.

Some trainers, unable to obtain the results they desire, resort to strong-arm tactics, forcing a horse to do their will by using ever-harsher bits and training devices, but not Millar. He prefers the repetition method of horse training: whatever the lesson may be, he repeats and repeats it until the horse accepts his guidance and gets the lesson down pat.

For example, a horse must learn to shorten stride when a rider requests it. The average-sized horses favoured for Grand Prix jumping will cover 11.5 to 13 feet in a cantering stride. Course designers take this into consideration when they set up obstacles for a competition, separating them by distances that are multiples of 13-foot strides and half strides. Big Ben cantered an 18-foot stride, so he had to learn to decrease his stride length to 13 feet or less when asked by his rider.

By using his weight, posture, and leg pressure against the horse's sides, the rider causes the horse to lift his head and neck, bring his hind legs farther under him, and move into the bit. This "collects" the horse and makes him shorten his stride. To lengthen the stride (extension), the rider encourages the horse to lower his head and neck and reach his forelegs farther forward.

Big Ben was a clever horse who knew exactly what he liked to do — and what he didn't like to do. If he didn't like to do something, he tried to evade it. Although he was a talented and powerful jumper, he didn't like some of the elements of basic schooling, such as learning to adjust his stride, so he would try to avoid doing it.

Millar didn't know it at the beginning of their relationship, but Big Ben also had exceptionally keen eyesight. This sometimes caused problems. At times, Millar thought Ben was using avoidance tactics when the horse was actually noticing something a distance away that flustered him. "He was not afraid; he fears few things," Millar explained in *Riding High*. "But allowing himself to be rattled ... was his method of evasion, his way of saying, 'I don't want to be trained, I don't want to be controlled'." With patience and persistence, Millar got him to respond.

Up Like a Rocket

The making of a top-notch jumping horse is a long and exacting process. The prospective champion is brought along slowly, and a horse aged 7 to 10 years old is often considered a "young" jumper.

A horse begins in the Preliminary class, where jumps are a maximum height of four feet, and advances through increasingly difficult divisions, with the jump heights raised progressively higher in each division, before finally arriving at the most difficult level, Grand Prix, with huge hurdles set at five feet three inches. This movement through the ranks can take 5, 7, or even 10 years, and riders don't hesitate to move their mounts back down in level if the horse's performance deteriorates after the advancement. Only a small number of horses reach the top, to become consistent winners.

In contrast, Big Ben's rise to show-jumping fame was meteoric. He competed in a small jumper show in Montreal, Quebec, in the spring of 1984. He did so well, Millar moved Ben up into the Preliminary class in Edmonton, Alberta, only one week later.

The horse was also successful in Edmonton: so much so that Millar entered him in the Open Jumper division in the same show the very next day. By the end of that week, Ben took on the Grand Prix division, posting a very creditable second-place finish. One week later, he won the Spruce Meadows Grand Prix. There was no stopping him! His show-jumping career took off like a rocket.

Ben was making a name for himself, and he was gaining fans from all over Canada. "Much of the fan mail addressed to Millar Brooke Farm is not for me at all," wrote Millar, "but for a horse named Ben. Big Ben." On average, he would get 10 to 12 fan letters per week, though later, when he became sick, fans sent him get-well cards by the hundreds.

Big Ben was so popular that people frequently asked for a few hairs from his mane or tail. If everyone who asked for hair had received a strand, poor Ben would have been as bald as an egg. To accommodate fans who begged for a memento of their favourite equine star, Sandi, his groom, would paint the horseshoe on Ben's front foot with ink and have him stand on a piece of paper, thereby signing his "autograph."

The horse was so popular that the Canadian Therapeutic Riding Association (CanTRA), which introduces people with physical and mental disabilities to riding as both sport and therapy, asked Ben to be their "poster horse" to help promote the group.

Tall and Short

Another amazing element in the unusual story of Big Ben is the relationship he had with his favourite groom, Sandi Patterson. Every horse has a person to whom it relates best, but the connection between Sandi and Big Ben appeared to be even stronger than normal.

Any picture of the two of them together shows a study in opposites: Sandi, the petite groom with a riot of strawberry blond locks, has the giant, dark horse stalking regally along behind, reminiscent of a trim little tugboat hauling a massive ocean liner in its wake.

At times, their relationship could be likened to that of a lowly servant (Sandi) at the beck and call of her master (Ben), dancing to his every whim. Sandi was

Ben's cleaning lady, tidying up his house — a huge box stall — every day. She was his dietician, bringing his four daily meals, which consisted of hay, hydroponically grown grass sprouts, or a specially mixed feed ration of bran, pellets, oats, molasses, and a touch of Metamucil to keep the horse's delicate digestive system chugging along properly.

The conscientious woman acted as a personal trainer, riding Ben for his daily exercise if Millar was away or otherwise unable to, and hand-walking him to keep him limber. Like a valet, she dressed him in his "clothes": saddles, bridles, protective leg boots, and blankets, keeping them clean and in good repair.

Sandi Patterson is short; her beloved charge was very tall. He had only to raise his head if he didn't want to be bridled, but because she was his greatest friend, Ben would almost always do what she asked him to do. When it was time for tacking up, he would submissively lower his head so she could bridle him.

She was Ben's personal care attendant, grooming and brushing him daily. She administered health treatments, operating an electromagnetic muscle relaxer and circulation stimulator for his back muscles. Big Ben also received laser treatments on key acupuncture points that were designed to relax other major muscles. Sandi did those treatments, too.

Sometimes she was his personal bodyguard, sleeping outside his stall in the horse-show barns, and at other times she was his appointments secretary, deciding when His Royal Highness would receive visitors and just who would be allowed to see him. With most grownups, he was blasé — if adult admirers came to see him in his stall at a show, he would usually pretend not to see them and turn away. But he loved children and would eagerly press his face against the bars so they could pet him.

Most of all, Sandi was his friend and companion, taking part in his antics when he was in a playful mood in the turnout paddock, or keeping him company by lying in the luxuriant green grass while he grazed nearby. While their interaction could be seen as that of a master and his servant, at other times it could only be described as a mutual admiration society, or even as an equine/human love match.

"When we first got him, Big Ben was not a people horse," explained Millar in *Riding High*. "He tolerated people because they fed him and brought him water, but he did not *like* people at all." Millar went on to recount that Patty Markell, Bobbie Donaher, Lori Green, and Sandi — the four people who looked after Ben over the years — were largely responsible for changing Ben's stand-offish behaviour.

"Does he love all people now?" Millar wrote in 1990. "No. He is not that type of horse. But, selectively, Big Ben really likes certain people, Sandi above all."

"I love him," Sandi said of her equine charge in Lawrence Scanlan's 1994 biography *Big Ben*. And the feeling, evidently, was reciprocated. "Ben will do anything for Sandi," said Millar's wife, Lynn, in Scanlan's book. "It's a matter of trust."

The King Has Quirks

No kings are completely faultless. They all have their idiosyncrasies, and Big Ben was no exception. Where other horses love apples, he detested them. His snack of choice was bran muffins, and adoring fans would send him muffins from all across the country.

He loved to play "catch the dandy brush" with Sandi Patterson and enjoyed playing the same game with young fans. He would hold the brush in his mouth, bob his head up, then open his mouth, and toss the brush to the delighted children. According to Sandi, Ben was a fine pitcher, but catching was beyond him.

More than a little like a spoiled child, Ben wanted what he wanted, and right now, please. "He's a horse with a lot of character. He thinks we are here to take care of him. He expects all the extras," Sandi told Lawrence Scanlan for *Big Ben*. "When he wants to go out, he wants to be first out and first ridden. If he's not ridden by 10 o'clock, he gets mad. He'll buck and twirl when it comes time to ride him. His electromagnetic machine has a buzzer that sounds when the time is up. When that buzzer goes, he wants off. Right away. He starts bobbing his head and pawing the ground."

Whenever Sandi had to leave Millar Brooke Farm for a few days, Ben would pout until she returned. Her return did not, however, let her off the hook. Ben would turn his back and ignore her, refusing to come to her, and grumping for days to show his displeasure at her absence.

He would not suffer even the slightest of discomforts with forbearance. Take flies, for instance. He didn't like the stable flies that would settle on his silken hide. Grant Cashmore, a New Zealander who stayed at Millar Brooke Farm for some instruction from Ian Millar, told Lawrence Scanlan about one day when he was out riding Big Ben. "All of a sudden he just stopped. There was a fly on his head. And he turned his head to look back at me, as if to say, 'Grant, would you swat that fly from my head, please?'"

Ian Millar got a hint of that sensitivity the first time he rode the horse during the pre-sale viewing. Millar used his own North American close-contact saddle; the European saddles that Ben was used to are not as flat, and they have more padding. When Millar's saddle was put on Ben, he showed his displeasure at the different feel by switching his tail and pinning back his ears with his head in the air.

"The minute I sat on him, I sensed that something was bothering him," Millar recalled in *Riding High.* "Wondering how the saddle fit, I put my finger under the front of it, only to find that it was too close to his withers. When I leaned forward the slightest bit, my weight pressed the front of the saddle down onto the wither bone ... Big Ben was *so* sensitive to this. Most horses, 99.9 percent of horses, would have tolerated this discomfort. Not Big Ben."

He would not even accept something as normal as an oral dewormer. These common paste-type concoctions kill parasites in a horse's digestive system. Ben didn't want it, and he simply raised his head so high that the grooms couldn't reach to put it in his mouth. Millar had to be cagey to combat the problem. He had Ben taken into a stable with a very low ceiling so the horse couldn't raise his head out of the way. Foiled again!

It often seemed there were no grey areas with this big horse, there was only black or white; he either liked something or he didn't. He *detested* green garbage bags because they might blow at him. They irked him so much that if he saw one when he was being ridden, he would buck and spin, succeeding on a couple of occasions in dumping Millar in the dirt.

Ben was definite about his creature comforts. In hot weather, he loved to have cold air blown on him with an electric fan. Weekly baths could be completed only if his rules were followed. It is common practice for grooms to secure a horse in cross-ties — fastening ropes on either side of a horse's halter with quick-release clips — before doing any kind of work on the animal. But of course, that's any *other* horse. Ben was an unusual case. If Sandi put him in cross-ties, he refused to lower his head so it could be bathed. His head would only come down when Sandi had removed the offending ropes.

Triple Threat

Big Ben could jump like a cat. Also like a cat, he seemed to have multiple lives, cheating death on three different occasions.

The digestive system of a horse is a delicate mechanism. When a horse has eaten too much — perhaps by overindulging on windfall apples, or after breaking into the feed bin and gorging himself — he cannot vomit. Whatever goes into the stomach must pass through the intestines and colon and be expelled as manure. If for some reason it *can't* pass through and forms a blockage, the result is a condition dreaded by all horse owners:

colic. Colic is one of the main causes of death in horses.

The pain of colic is so intense that a horse will often throw himself to the stall floor and roll back and forth, trying to relieve the pain. The danger of this action is that the violent rolling can cause a twist in the bowels, which cuts off the blood supply to a section of the intestine. Without its steady supply of oxygen-rich blood, the affected part of the intestine will begin to die. If the condition is left untreated, the horse will likely die, too.

Big Ben may have been a superhorse in many ways, but he was no more immune to colic than any other equine. In March 1990, the Millar horses were in Florida for a competition. They were staying at a stable in Tampa. The sun was spilling through the trees on a warm, bright day, but a dark shadow was cast inside the barn. Ben began exhibiting signs of colic, pawing the ground and walking around and around in his stall.

Attending veterinarian Dr. Rick Mitchell told Ian that the problem was an impaction. He began treating the distressed Ben with intravenous fluids and anti-inflammatory drugs, hoping the impaction would pass. The treatment seemed to be working, but all anyone could do was watch and wait. Sandi kept Ben company; it helped to pass the time.

Suddenly, around suppertime, the mighty horse thudded to the stall floor, like a massive oak felled by the woodsman's axe, and began to thrash back and forth. In spite of her fright and the danger from his flailing hooves, Sandi dashed in to try to get Ben up and walking. Stopping a horse from rolling and keeping him walking often help to get things moving along inside.

Getting a colicky horse up is difficult. You may have to tug and pull at him because he hurts, and he doesn't *want* to get up. In some cases where the horse is very stubborn or reluctant, attendants may have to swat him with a broom, or bang a stick on a metal bucket to frighten him. However she managed it, Sandi got Ben to his feet.

She was walking Ben in the arena when Dr. Mitchell and Millar charged back into the barn. They decided to take the horse to the clinic in Ocala, Florida, about one and a half hours away, posthaste. Dr. Don Sloan advised immediate surgery; however, Millar wanted to wait just a little longer to see if the situation would possibly resolve itself. It did not. By 6:30 the next morning, Dr. Sloan was preparing to take Ben to surgery.

Colic surgery is tough on a horse. On average, the survival rate for a less severe colic surgery is 85 percent. Horses that need to have a portion of their small intestine removed face only a 65 percent chance of surviving. Most horses take months to recover, and few ever compete successfully again following their convalescence.

Dr. Sloan began the surgery and found where the blockage was. He got it to move by injecting it with saline. Luckily, he was able to avoid cutting into Ben's intestine. He advised the Millars of possible complications from colic surgery and told them, "You're not even close to being out of the woods yet. Not for six weeks, anyway." Sloan prescribed a detailed plan for Ben's recovery: constant light exercise for weeks, being led at a walk every day.

Ben recuperated far more quickly than the clinic staff anticipated. They were amazed and credited his quick convalescence to his high level of conditioning. Approximately 12 weeks after his surgery, Big Ben won the Grand Prix at the Spruce Meadows National. He was back — and as good as ever. But the shadow returned.

In the early hours of a cold January morning in 1991, Sandi Patterson found Ben walking his stall, stopping now and again to paw at the ground. His morning ration lay uneaten — never a good sign. Her heart dropped to her toes as she faced the possibility that the great horse was again colicking. She quickly summoned the husband-and-wife veterinarian team of John Atack and Linda Berthiaume, who have an equine clinic right on Millar Brooke Farm.

Ian and Lynn Millar were in New York on a horse-buying foray, 10 hours away. Sandi was finally able to contact them mid-morning to give them the sombre news. Millar spoke with Dr. Atack, who assured him everything that could be done was being done. "If he doesn't improve soon, Ian," Atack said, "we'll take him to the clinic at the University of Guelph." (Atack was referring to the Ontario Veterinary College clinic, which is at the university.)

For 90 minutes, Atack bombarded the blockage with all the standard treatments: oils, fluids, and walking. None of them worked. After tranquillizing Big Ben and giving him a painkiller, Atack had the horse loaded into a van for the six-and-a-half-hour trip to Guelph. Sandi was at Ben's side in the trailer, offering comfort and support.

It was early evening by the time they pulled into the clinic's admitting area. They had had to stop about 30 kilometres out so that Atack could give Ben another needle to ease his terrible pain.

Dr. Ron Trout was the surgeon on call that night. He assessed Big Ben's condition: high heart rate (which indicates pain), bloated belly, and a seriously swollen large intestine. All symptoms indicated that immediate surgery was imperative.

The big gelding was taken directly to the pre-op, where he was prepped and given anesthetic. Almost instantaneously, he slumped to the floor, which is in fact an operating table that is raised and lowered by hydraulics. Technicians shaved his belly and a patch on his neck, and then, to reduce the possibility of infection from contamination, they wrapped his hooves with plastic covers before draping green surgical sheets over his body and wheeling him into surgery.

Sandi viewed the whole operation on a TV monitor and watched as Dr. Trout found the blockage in Ben's grossly swollen intestine. As the vet had done during Ben's previous colic surgery, Trout injected a salt solution into the blockage. This made it wetter and allowed the vet to massage and thin it out. "Then he stopped," wrote Lawrence Scanlan in *Big Ben*, "confident that nature — Big Ben's own horse plumbing — would move it all out later. Had the surgeon been forced to remove the blockage by cutting into the intestine, the odds of recovery would have declined, for the chance of infection would have risen."

Big Ben had already beaten the odds by surviving not one, but two colic surgeries in less than a year. That was astounding in and of itself, but horses who survive colic surgery rarely, if ever, return to the same level of proficiency they were at prior to the operation. It is even more unlikely the older the horse is. Ben was now 15 years old. Was his career over?

Happily, it wasn't. Later that year, Ben won the

du Maurier International, the richest event at Spruce Meadows, for the second time and also helped Canada win the Nations Cup at the Royal Winter Fair. It looked like he could go on competing and winning forever. But his trials were not yet over.

Highway of Horror
When Millar Brooke Farm horses commute to shows in North America, they travel in sleek silver-grey and blue horse trailers, pulled by semi-trucks. Horses face some exhaustingly long road trips because Air Canada deemed horse air transport within Canada unprofitable and discontinued it.

It was nearing midnight on May 24, 1992, and Big Ben was ensconced in his favourite stall, behind the driver's seat, as he had been on many a trip before. The gelding dozed as the rig conveyed him and seven equine compatriots through the Saskatchewan countryside on a rainy night. Their destination: Edmonton, a 57-hour trip from home. It was only the first stop on the competition trail. From there it was on to Calgary for a week-long tournament before heading back home to Ontario.

Sandi Patterson was in the passenger seat of the truck cab, her shoes off so she was more comfortable. She drifted in and out of sleep, while Ken Armstrong was at the wheel. They were in the lead, with other grooms following in passenger vehicles, and behind them, two more horse transports.

Suddenly, a vehicle going the opposite direction sped out of the night towards them. The pair in the truck cab saw with horror that it was in their lane — they were on a collision course! Armstrong made a valiant effort to avoid the vehicle, but the metal missile, travelling at 100 kilometres per hour, smashed into the front axle of the truck and burst into flames.

Without its axle, the mangled horse van became a lumbering elephant, out of control. Down the highway it slid, sideways, then headed for the ditch, where it teetered onto its right side in slow motion.

Neither Patterson nor Armstrong was seriously hurt, but Armstrong was unable to get out: his legs were pinned. Since the passenger door was jammed into the dirt, Sandi had to get out the driver's side door, which she had to reach by crawling over Armstrong.

Opening the door was a challenge. Sandi had to push it upwards, like opening the trapdoor into an attic. Truck doors are extremely heavy, and it was all she could do to hold the door open long enough for her to squeeze out of the crippled vehicle.

She sprinted down the length of the trailer, her bare feet splashing in puddles and in danger of being slashed to pieces by broken glass from the accident. She scaled the side of the toppled van to find the loading door, then struggled to get it open and look inside the trailer.

Blessedly, the lights inside the horse trailer were still working, and Sandi could see the terror-stricken horses struggling to stand upright. Since the side of the transport was now the floor, their legs flailed about, trying to gain a purchase on metal walls with their metal-shod feet. Uppermost in Sandi's mind was the need to get Ben and the other horses out. But the accident had jammed the back door shut.

Two Millar Brooke grooms who had been driving directly behind the lead truck came rushing to help. They had narrowly missed hitting both the mini-van that caused the accident and the semi-truck's front axle, which the impact had dislodged. But there was little any of them could do. They needed help, and they needed it quickly. They flagged down a passing motorist and asked him to call for fire trucks, ambulance, and police. Sandi and the other grooms tried to rescue the mini-van's driver, but the fiercely burning flames drove them back.

Meanwhile, the horses were still panicking inside the trailer. One horse had been instantly killed in the accident; another, Baarlo, had fallen under the hooves of one of the other six remaining live horses.

Within 30 minutes, ambulances, attendants, firefighters, and fire trucks began arriving to assist the victims. They released Ken Armstrong from the wreckage and took him to the hospital. It was too late for the mini-van driver, who had died in the crash or the resulting fire. Now, all eyes turned to the horses.

It is not unusual for horses to survive an accident, only to bolt in panic from the scene and be struck by another passing vehicle, or go into shock afterwards and die. If there was any blessing in such a horrific collision, it was that the horses were still contained and safe from traffic. But with the back doors jammed shut, how would the rescuers get them out?

Using a crowbar — and their hands — to tear holes in the roof (now the side) of the van, Sandi and the others worked frantically to strip back a section of the roof to create a hole big enough for the horses to be brought out.

Big Ben had battered the trailer's side with his head until he poked a hole through the metal. He now sported a bad cut over his right eye. The rescuers led him out first, then they brought out the rest of the horses.

Generous and sympathetic horse owners at the Rusty Spurs Equestrian Centre made space for the original passengers of the second horse transport. Then the driver loaded Big Ben and the other injured horses and took them to the nearby Saskatoon Equine Clinic.

Besides the cut over his eye, which needed stitches, Big Ben had cuts on his legs and an abrasion on his nose. A couple of the other horses were cut by broken glass: Gusty Munroe on the knee, and Future Vision on one of his hocks. Baarlo, who initially seemed to have only minor cuts and bruises, even after he had been stood on for so long, took over a year to recover from damage to his back.

The injured horses, none of whom ultimately competed at the Edmonton show, were rested at Rusty Spurs for a week before being taken home. Being in or around trailers spooked them for months afterwards. But Big Ben was a trooper. Two weeks after the accident, he won all three classes in which he was entered at Calgary's Spruce Meadows, including a Grand Prix. It's difficult to keep a good horse down!

King of the Ring

Even after two bouts with colic and a horrifying traffic accident, Ben continued to compete successfully at the top levels. One of his favourite places was Spruce Meadows, which could have been called his second home. There he racked up more repeat wins than any other horse in history. It was the scene of some of his most impressive triumphs, perhaps because the course is ideally suited to big, ground-covering horses like Ben.

Fans by the thousands attend Spruce Meadows' big events. They sit on the grass on the viewing bank and cheer on their favourites. Big Ben and Ian Millar frequently drew the loudest cheers.

One of Big Ben's most memorable traits was his ability to go into the ring, jump every jump clean, without seeming to hurry, and yet cross the finish line, stopping the time clock, a fraction of a second faster than his closest competitors, wresting the victory from their grasp. He was a master at the timed jump-off.

So clever was he, and so fast and agile, that he could often snatch victory from seeming defeat. In the 1991 Nations Cup at Spruce Meadows, Ben approached an obstacle and soared into the air. While still airborne, but beginning his descent, he realized that the obstacle was not a single upright but a spread jump, with another set of rails in front of him. Even though his front legs had started to come down between the two fences, he was able to gather himself, tuck the legs back up, stretch out, and clear the second bar without knocking down either element. He pulled off a clean round and helped the Canadian team win the event.

The Spruce Meadows Derby is a longer course than a regular Grand Prix class: it is a real test of stamina, and clear rounds have been rare. In 1993, Ben triumphed in the Spruce Meadows Derby for an unprecedented sixth time, and for the third consecutive year.

"No other horse has come close to matching that achievement," wrote Lawrence Scanlan. "Big Ben took every jump in the derby before knocking down the very last one. This forced a jump-off against two other horses, which he narrowly won. Big Ben's record at Spruce Meadows in Calgary may never be duplicated."

In his book *Riding High*, Ian Millar said, "Two or three years at the top is all you can expect from horses competing at the grand prix level." Guess he never told Big Ben that! With over 100 wins and a total of $1.5 million in prize money garnered in a career that lasted over 11 years, Big Ben was, indeed, King of the Ring.

Last Days

In 1994, Ian Millar decided it was time for Big Ben to retire. Millar wanted his partner to bid farewell to the game while he was still at the top. The pair went on an eight-city farewell tour. Ben's fans were so eager to see him that thousands of them stood in line for several hours at each stop for a chance to say goodbye.

Ben returned to Millar Brooke Farm in Perth, Ontario, where he lived the life of luxury and ease that he so greatly deserved, with Sandi lovingly attending to his needs, as always.

In December 1999, the dark shadow of colic stole

into Ben's life for the third and final time. He had beaten the odds twice before and survived the scourge of the stable, but he was now 23 years old, an equine senior citizen. His valiant, inextinguishable spirit was growing tired, too weary to fight any longer.

When Ben developed colic on Friday evening, December 10, Dr. John Atack, his longtime veterinarian, struggled throughout the night to save him. However, in the early morning hours of December 11, Atack recommended that Big Ben be euthanized to relieve his suffering.

"He was in pain. They were at the stage of using very serious drugs to keep the pain under control," said Ian Millar in an interview in the *Ottawa Citizen* on December 12, 1999. "It was a very difficult decision."

Horse lovers around the world mourned the loss of Big Ben. The Canadian Therapeutic Riding Association (CanTRA), which received contributions in his memory, pays tribute to the gelding on its web site: "When Big Ben died in December 1999, the Canadian Therapeutic Riding Association lost a beloved friend and ambassador. He and Ian Millar were supporters of CanTRA for over 10 years, helping to raise awareness of the benefits of therapeutic riding through public appearances, a promotional video and the Big Ben Retirement Tour."

Big Ben is buried on Millar Brooke Farm, in a spot

overlooking the barns and training area. He may be gone, but he certainly isn't forgotten. As well as being a goodwill ambassador and poster horse for CanTRA, he was immortalized forever by Reeves International, a toy manufacturing company in the United States, which moulds millions of plastic horse figurines of all types and breeds.

He has been commemorated on a postage stamp by Canada Post, was made an honorary member of the RCMP Musical Ride, was inducted into the Ontario Sports Legends Hall of Fame, and, along with Northern Dancer, a famous Canadian Thoroughbred race horse, was one of only two non-human entries inducted into the Canadian Sports Hall of Fame.

Images of Ben in competition are etched forever in the memories of show-jumping fans. They can still see the tall chestnut with his head high and proud, and his tail arched. They remember how he would stride regally into the ring, his head turning and bowing from side to side like a monarch on royal parade, deigning to notice his lowly subjects. The "un-h, un-h" vocalization he made while cantering, which got louder as the competition became more intense, lingers in their ears.

This noise turned out to be not a breathing problem at all, as was assumed by so many of the prospective buyers who passed up the gelding. Instead, it was another individual quirk. It may be fanciful, but to some, Ben's chuffing noise appeared to be a self-motivational tool, his own version of the Little Engine That Could's "I know I can, I know I can ..."

Big Ben, the tall and gangly chestnut gelding from Belgium, the gelding nobody wanted, successfully made the transition from commoner to show-ring king, transformed by the patience and skill of Ian Millar, just as an unremarkable lump of carbon is transformed into a priceless diamond by the skill of a diamond cutter. He will live on in the hearts and minds of those who loved him.

Reign forever, Big Ben!

Glossary

Appaloosa: A horse breed characterized by its colourful spotted coat. Originally bred by the Nez Perce Indians in their lands around the Palouse River in the Pacific Northwest, the Appaloosa has five recognized coat patterns: frost, marble, snowflake, and the two most common, blanket and leopard spotted.

Bay: A brown coat colour (can range from deep reddish-brown to dark brown) with black mane, tail, and legs.

Blood horse: An old-time term used to describe a saddle horse or race horse of fine breeding, rather than a mixed-breed animal.

Bog-spavin: A soft swelling on the hock that can be caused by conformation fault, a strain from quick turning and fast stops, or deficiencies in vitamins A and D, calcium, and phosphorus.

Box stall: A large (usually 10 foot by 10 foot square), four-sided stall in which the horse is not tied and can move around freely, as opposed to a straight stall, which is narrower (approximately 5 feet by 10 feet), three sided, and in which the horse is tied.

Brush and mask (of a fox): The brush is another word for the tail; the mask is the fox's head or face.

Cavalletti: A small wooden jumping pole with X-shaped ends, which can be adjusted in height. They are used to train horses and riders beginning to learn jumping.

Chestnut: A reddish coat colour. The mane and tail are usually the same colour as the coat.

Dandy brush: A grooming brush with stiff, upstanding bristles. Used with short, sharp, flick-of-the-wrist action to remove dirt from the horse's coat.

Draw: To send hounds into woods or brush to find a fox.

Fault: A penalty assessed in jumper classes for mistakes such as knockdowns, refusals, and exceeding the time allowed to complete the course.

Godolphin Arabian: One of the three foundation sires of the Thoroughbred breed.

Hack: A horse available for hire, used in all kinds of service, or a horse worn out from overuse. Also, to ride or drive for pleasure, as opposed to working, i.e., racing, hunting, etc.

Hacking: A ride for pleasure, rather than for training the horses. A relaxing ride at a walk, trot, and/or slow canter.

Hock: The large bony joint on a horse's hind leg, connecting the upper and lower leg bones.

Knockdown: An obstacle is considered knocked down when a horse or rider, by contact, lowers any element that establishes the height of an obstacle. However, if the horse hits a bar and it jumps up in the air and falls back on the jump cups again, no faults are incurred.

Refusal: If a horse stops before a jump or ducks out to the side to keep from going over the jump, officials consider that a refusal. A refusal usually gives a horse four faults.

Two-point position: A riding position assumed in jumping, in which the rider's legs are against the horse's sides, with the posterior lifted up off the saddle, and the rider rising from his or her knees.

Warmblood: The term used to describe equines developed by crossing cold-blooded horses (the heavy draft breeds) with hot-blooded horses (Thoroughbreds, Arabians, etc.). Over the years, these crosses have produced "warmblooded" breeds like the Trakehner, Hanoverian, and Friesian.

Bibliography

Scanlan, Lawrence. *Big Ben*. Richmond Hill, ON: Scholastic Canada, 1994.

May, Zita Barbara. *Canada's International Equestrians*. Toronto: Burns and MacEachern, 1975.

Millar, Ian, and Larry Scanlan. *Riding High: Ian Millar's World of Show Jumping*. Toronto: McClelland and Stewart, 1990.

Bolte, Betty. *Jumping*. Chelsea House Publishing, 2001. Draper, Judith. *Show Jumping Records, Facts and Champions*. Sterling Publishing Company, Incorporated, 1988.

Draper, Judith. *The Stars of Show Jumping*. Trafalgar Square, 1991.

Furth, Elizabeth. *Visions of Show Jumping*. The Lyons Press, 2000.

Martin, Ann. *Masters of Show Jumping.* Hungry Minds, Inc., 1991.

Hale, Cindy, and Sharon P. Fibelkorn. *Riding for the Blue: A Celebration of Horse Shows.* Bow Tie Press, 2003.

Acknowledgments

The author acknowledges the following sources for the quotes contained in this book: the historical book *Memory Meadows* by Grant MacEwan; the in-depth chronicle authored by Zita Barbara May, *Canada's International Equestrians*; Larry Scanlan's overview of Big Ben in his book of the same name; Ian Millar's autobiography, *Riding High: Ian Millar's World of Show Jumping*, which he co-authored with Larry Scanlan. For additional information the author referred to the following texts: *The Eyewitness Handbook for Horses* by Elwyn Harley Edwards, *Guide to Horses of the World* by Treasure Press, and *Basic Training for Horses: English and Western* by Eleanor F. Prince and Gaydell M. Collier.

Thanks also to the staff of the Stockman's Memorial Foundation of Cochrane, Alberta, who were invaluable in rooting out information when it eluded me. They were able to supply copies of articles from *Horse & Rodeo*, vol. 1, no. 2 (July 1962), and *Golden West* magazine (Summer 1977). As well, thanks to Mrs. Yogi Fell of South Granville, Prince Edward Island, a veritable fountain of horse knowledge, as well as to the members of the Canadian Model HorseNet, for their combined equine information. And, of course, to Audrey McClellan, editor extraordinaire and fellow horseman.

In addition, thanks to Alberta Equine On-Line, CBC Sports Online, Canadian Encyclopedia Online, the Canadian Therapeutic Riding Association (CanTRA), the *Chronicle of the Horse*, HickokSports.com, Horse-Canada.com, The Horse.com, the International Museum of the Horse, the Masters of Foxhounds Association of America, the Glossary of Horse Terms, Ohio State University (Bulletin 762-00 on Horse Nutrition), Sporting Origins, Spruce Meadows, and the World Olympians Education, for the information and quotes found on their web sites.

Photo Credits

About the Author

Debbie Gamble-Arsenault has been horse mad since she was a toddler; family rumour has it that "horse" was practically the first word she spoke.

Raised in a close-knit, loving family, long on children, but short on horses, she fed her passion for equines by collecting model horse figurines (a collection that now numbers over 800), reading horse stories, and begging rides on neighbourhood farm horses.

It seemed only natural that horses would be the first topic she wrote about when she began her writing career over 25 years ago. Since then, she has been published in numerous periodicals and newspapers across North America on a wide range of topics. This is her first book.

Debbie lives in Alexandra, a rural community on the outskirts of Charlottetown, Prince Edward Island, with her husband, Tim Arsenault, and two furry cat-children. Her hobbies include reading prodigiously, model horse collecting and showing, motorcycle touring and attending rallies, and having "tea and chat" with her friends.

The author is active in her church and Women's

Institute, as well as other community-service organizations. She is a charter member of the Island Writer's Association and has been a member of the Periodical Writer's Association of Canada for more than 15 years.

Debbie Gamble-Arsenault loves to hear from her readers. She may be reached at: 1320 Pownal Road; R.R.#1, (Alexandra); Charlottetown, PEI, C1A 7J6, or by e-mail at: dgamble@isn.net

AMAZING STORIES™

THE HEART OF A HORSE

Poignant Tales and Humorous Escapades

ANIMAL/HUMAN INTEREST
by Gayle Bunney

ISBN 1-55153-994-2

AMAZING STORIES™

STOLEN HORSES

Tales of Modern-Day Horse Rustling

ANIMAL/CRIME

by Dorothy Pedersen

ISBN 1-55153-971-3

AMAZING STORIES™

WILDERNESS TALES

Adventures in the Backcountry

HUMAN INTEREST/BACKCOUNTRY
by Peter Christensen

ISBN 1-55153-987-X

AMAZING STORIES™

GREAT DOG STORIES

Inspirational Tales About
Exceptional Dogs

ANIMAL/HUMAN INTEREST

by Roxanne Willems Snopek

ISBN 1-55153-946-2

OTHER AMAZING STORIES

These titles are available wherever you buy books. If you have trouble finding the book you want, call the Altitude order desk at 1-800-957-6888, e-mail your request to: orderdesk@altitudepublishing.com or visit our Web site at www.amazingstories.ca

New AMAZING STORIES titles are published every month. If you would like more information, e-mail your name and mailing address to: amazingstories@altitudepublishing.com.